Praise for *The Leaд.. ⎯ ⎯*
to Impact

'Leadership and impact are associated so strongly in this book, by showing how thoughtful leadership behaviours impact business results, which is music to the ears of an action-oriented leader. It has a very practical approach, which makes it easy to read and actionable. The language is different from the often too theoretical language used; it is more suited to the language leaders use in their day-to-day communication.'

Carlo Enrico, President LAC, Mastercard

'A thought-provoking book on the human-to-human impact that we make a thousand times a day and how to think about improving this impact without forgetting to always be our (non-"greenwashed") selves!'

Ken Stannard, CEO, Cabot Credit Management

'For aspiring life guards this book is a must-read on how to give oxygen to create energy and have impact (like JR). This book is for anyone who wants to breathe life into their team through inspiration resulting in impact, leading to higher engagement, better customer experience and, ultimately, revenue.'

Neal Watkins, Chief Product Officer and Executive Board Director, BAE Systems Applied Intelligence, UK

'If there is one book you read on leadership, this is it. It's jam packed with practical tips, stories and frameworks to help you to be the best leader you can possibly be by taking control of your impact on those around you. Elisabet and

Mandy hit the leadership nail on the head every time! I wish this book was around 20 years ago!'

Vanessa Vallely, OBE, Managing Director, WeAreTheCity; author, *Heels of Steel*

'Explodes the myth that leaders are born, not made. Part art, part science; effective leadership – as this book proves – is 100 per cent about practice, practice, practice.'

Tom Derry, CEO, Institute for Supply Management

'A compelling read for these disruptive times – as relevant to the C-suite occupant as it is for the new team leader.'

Ian Holden-Semple, executive with 30 years operations experience in financial services including global banking, card payments and insurance

'You know a book is great when from page one it feels connected to where you are and what you need right now. I was able to use ideas from the book straight away and the balance of research, ideas and case studies has given me a deeper understanding of how impact is created in those daily choices, both my own and that of those around me. I highly recommend this book to leaders of all levels; this kind of insight is invaluable.'

Lizzie Smith, Local Director, Health Education England, London

'A great book on how to become an even better leader in today's complex work environment, where our ability to have an impact is more important than ever in order to be successful. A must-read if you want to move your career to the next stage.'

Nick Shaw, Vice President and GM Consumer Symantec EMEA

'Impact is such an important and not really talked about topic. This book shows that impact starts from within, and there are many good examples and situations that I could relate to. I immediately started to evaluate and consider my own impact from the moment I walked in the front door at home to read it, to walking into the office the following day.'

Tim Noble, Vice President, Global Head of Sales,
ICE Data Services

'In *The Leader's Guide to Impact,* Mandy and Elisabet share their rich insights from years of coaching executives and teams. They provide actions and models you can use TODAY to raise your impact as a leader.'

John Turner, Chief Revenue Officer, Chronicle
(an Alphabet Company)

'I felt the book to be "on point" and relevant to current agile fast flowing and complex projects (with multiple hierarchy of stakeholders and colleagues) whilst enabling me to consider brand and reputation whilst balancing stakeholders, culture and collaboration.'

Theresa Sayers, Chartered MCIPD, Tri Force ERP Project:
Surrey, Sussex and Thames Valley Police

'An eye-opening book with key analogies helping us understand the intricacies and importance of impact and influence. A must-read for any business owner or entrepreneur.'

Josh Wilson, Founder and MD, Wilson Worldwide
Productions, *Forbes 30 under 30*

'After 30 years in business, I cannot think of a leader who wouldn't benefit from the lessons in this book. An exceptional guide to creating the impact you want while enjoying the rewards that will follow.'

Chris Cooper, Business Engagement and Elevation; author;
speaker; host of *The Business Elevation Show* on Voice
America Business

'A fun and different leadership book, full of stories, opportunities for reflection and concrete solutions to apply. I really recommend this book to all leaders. I got so many new insights. I'm humbled and see new opportunities with my leadership which makes me truly inspired.'

Marie Lundström, Identity Leader Global Marketing Communication, Inter-IKEA Systems

'As always, I find Elisabet and Mandy's books on point for what is relevant in today's organisations and what is going on for me personally as a leader. I have been thinking a lot about mindfulness and my impact in the organisation, and this book provides an action plan around what I dubbed as #mindfulleadership. Additionally, Elisabet and Mandy do a wonderful job of creating do-it-yourself tools that take the guesswork out of creating action plans, whether personal or organisational. Thank you Elisabet and Mandy.'

Dena Bobolos, Senior banking leader with over 20 years of international experience, USA

The Leader's Guide to Impact

Pearson

At Pearson, we have a simple mission: to help people make more of their lives through learning.

We combine innovative learning technology with trusted content and educational expertise to provide engaging and effective learning experiences that serve people wherever and whenever they are learning.

From classroom to boardroom, our curriculum materials, digital learning tools and testing programmes help to educate millions of people worldwide – more than any other private enterprise.

Every day our work helps learning flourish, and wherever learning flourishes, so do people.

To learn more, please visit us at **www.pearson.com/uk**

The Leader's Guide to Impact

How to use soft skills to get hard results

Mandy Flint
Elisabet Vinberg Hearn

 Pearson

Harlow, England • London • New York • Boston • San Francisco • Toronto • Sydney • Dubai • Singapore • Hong Kong
Tokyo • Seoul • Taipei • New Delhi • Cape Town • São Paulo • Mexico City • Madrid • Amsterdam • Munich • Paris • Milan

PEARSON EDUCATION LIMITED

KAO Two
KAO Park
Harlow CM17 9SR
United Kingdom
Tel: +44 (0)1279 623623
Web: www.pearson.com/uk

First edition published 2019 (print and electronic)
© Pearson Education Limited 2019 (print and electronic)

ISBN: 978-1-292-24377-1 (print)
         978-1-292-24378-8 (PDF)
         978-1-292-24379-5 (ePub)

British Library Cataloguing-in-Publication Data
A catalogue record for the print edition is available from the British Library

Library of Congress Cataloging-in-Publication Data
A catalog record for the print edition is available from the Library of Congress

10 9 8 7 6 5 4 3 2 1
23 22 21 20 19

Print edition typeset in Melior Com 9/13 by Pearson CSC.
Printed by Ashford Colour Press Ltd, Gosport

NOTE THAT ANY PAGE CROSS REFERENCES REFER TO THE PRINT EDITION

Contents

About the authors

Mandy Flint is an international expert on leadership, leading teams and cultural behavioural change. Mandy is the CEO of Excellence in Leadership, a global transformational change organisation which she founded in 2000 after over 20 years of leadership experience in the corporate world. During this time, Mandy spent 14 years working for American Express, leading business units, and held roles in sales operations, public affairs, communications and cultural change.

As well as leading a business division within American Express as a senior leader, Mandy spent three years leading a cultural change transformation programme for the President as well as operating as an internal coach and team coach to many senior executives and teams.

Through Excellence in Leadership, Mandy works across the globe with both teams and individuals in the areas of one-to-one executive coaching, group facilitation, team effectiveness, vision creation, strategic development and cultural change leadership, working at an emotional and behavioural level. Her clients include CEOs, SVPs, VPs and board members in many multinational blue-chip organisations. Mandy has worked with a variety of companies including MasterCard, Lloyds, American Express, Symantec, Virgin Atlantic, Hewlett Packard, SAP, the NHS and BAE Systems.

Mandy studied at Harvard Business School, focusing on the concept of the Service Profit Chain. She is also media-trained and is an established speaker on leadership and cultural change. She is a fellow at the London Metropolitan Business School and has co-authored with Elisabet two multi-award-winning books on leadership and teams.

Elisabet Vinberg Hearn is a speaker, author, leadership strategist and executive coach, specialising in future leadership, winning teams, culture transformation and business sustainability. She is CEO of Katapult Partners Ltd, and co-founder of Think Solutions. Katapult, as an extension of Think's successful formula, focuses on the powerful role of leadership and culture in *digital transformations* specifically.

Before setting up Think Solutions in 2001, Elisabet worked internationally at American Express for 13 years, where she held various leadership roles, responsible for customer servicing, process re-engineering and corporate culture transformation.

Elisabet works with organisations around the world, providing strategic leadership and tactical solutions; facilitating organisational transformation, coaching and working with executives, leadership teams, digital transformation leaders and other change champions. Her experience spans diverse industries, with clients such as ABN AMRO, Royal Bank of Scotland, American Express, H&M, IKEA, Skanska, Vattenfall, Trygg-Hansa (Royal Sun Alliance), SOS Children's Villages and Greenpeace.

She has an MBA in Leadership and Sustainability from the University of Cumbria and a degree in Marketing Economics from IHM Business School, Stockholm. Together with Mandy, Elisabet is a published author of the multi-award winning books *The Team Formula: A Leadership Tale of a Team Who Found Their Way* and *Leading Teams – 10 Challenges: 10 Solutions.*

Acknowledgements

There are a number of people we want to thank and acknowledge in helping us to make this, our third book, a reality.

Thanks to all our clients, colleagues and teams who continue to inspire us and make us want to share our experience and insights and write these books.

Thank you to our editor Eloise Cook at Pearson Education for asking us to write this book; thanks for your ongoing support and guidance.

Our continued thanks to Barbara Large for her inspiration and for helping us on our route to book writing.

As always, we have had the constant support of our family and friends; we are so grateful for all your support – thank you.

Publisher's acknowledgements

Text credits

3 O.C. Tanner Learning Group: O.C. Tanner Learning Group, https://www.octanner.com/content/dam/oc-tanner/documents/global-research/White_Paper_Performance_Accelerated.pdf **3 Oxford University Press:** Oxford Dictionaries **9 Maya Angelou:** Maya Angelou **21 Harvard Business School Publishing:** https://hbr.org/2016/01/the-trickle-down-effect-of-good-and-bad-leadership **23 Gallup, Inc.:** http://news.gallup.com/businessjournal/182792/

managers-account-variance-employee-engagement.aspx
23 Gallup, Inc.: http://news.gallup.com/businessjournal/
163130/employee-engagement-drives-growth.aspx **24 Les
Brown:** Les Brown **25 The Misfits Media Company Pty
Limited:** Levo Institute, http://www.bandt.com.au/opinion/
five-reasons-emotional-intelligence-essential-effective-
leadership **41 Gloria Steinem:** Gloria Steinem **48 Guardian
News and Media Limited:** https://www.theguardian.com/
careers/careers-blog/what-employees-want-job-company-
around-world **66 Sheryl Sandberg:** Sheryl Sandberg **67 Gallup,
Inc.:** Gallup/Bain & Company, https://hbr.org/2015/12/
engaging-your-employees-is-good-but-dont-stop-there
75 Mind Tools Ltd: Mindtools.com **90 Anita Roddick.:**
Anita Roddick **91 Gallup, Inc.:** https://www.gallup.com/
workplace/236570/employees-lot-managers.aspx **103 Pearson
Education:** Leading Teams - 10 Challenges: 10 Solutions,
Mandy Flint, Elisabet Vinberg Hearn, FT Publishing
International, 978-1-292-08308-7. **112 Development
Dimensions International, Inc:** Global Leadership Forecast,
https://www.ddiworld.com/glf2018 **138 James Humes:**
James Humes **139 Weber Shandwick, Inc.:** https://www.
webershandwick.com/news/81-percent-of-global-executives-
report-external-ceo-engagement-is-a-mandate/ **145 Mansueto
Ventures:** https://www.inc.com/justin-bariso/uber-ceo-single-
insulting-tweet-destroy-months-work-major-lesson-emotional-
intelligence.html **152 Pearson Education:** Leading Teams - 10
Challenges: 10 Solutions, Mandy Flint, Elisabet Vinberg Hearn,
FT Publishing International, 978-1-292-08308-7. **159 Benjamin
Franklin:** Benjamin Franklin **163 The New York Times
Company:** https://www.nytimes.com/2016/02/28/magazine/
what-google-learned-from-its-quest-to-build-the-perfect-
team.html **190 Thomas Stallkamp:** Thomas Stallkamp
191 Development Dimensions International, Inc.,: https://
www.ddiworld.com/glf/gender-diversity-pays-off **228 Stephen
Hawking:** Stephen Hawking **229 O.C. Tanner Learning Group:**
https://www.octanner.com/in/insights/infographics/the-
business-case-for-recognition.html **256 Harvard Business**

School Publishing: https://hbr.org/2018/07/the-biggest-obstacles-to-innovation-in-large-companies **263 Alan Kay:** Alan Kay (1971) at a 1971 meeting of PARC **264 Development Dimensions International, Inc.,:** https://www.ddiworld.com/glf2018 **269 United Nations:** https://www.un.org/sustainabledevelopment/news/communications-material/. **280 Pearson Education:** Leading Teams - 10 Challenges: 10 Solutions, Mandy Flint, Elisabet Vinberg Hearn, FT Publishing International, 978-1-292-08308-7. **294 Marc Benioff:** with permission.

Photo credits

11 Mandy Flint: with permission **12 Elisabet Vinberg Hearn:** with permission **105 Pearson Education:** Amit John/Pearson India Education Services Pvt. Ltd **105 Shutterstock:** insima/Shutterstock **105 Pearson Education:** Ratan Mani Banerjee/Pearson India Education Services Pvt. Ltd **105 Pearson Education:** Arvind Singh Negi/Red Reef Design Studio/Pearson India Education Services Pvt. Ltd **184 MX publishing:** "The Team Formula: The Leadership Tale of a Team who found their Way" published by MX publishing 2013. ISBN-10: 1780923473

Introduction

Congratulations on choosing to read this book. You are taking an intentional approach to your impact.

What impact are you having on people and the world around you?

We cannot know for sure, but, as this book has caught your attention, we can assume you know how important impact is and you probably want to maximise your impact in a positive and results-driven way.

As a leader, you deliver results with and through others and, as such, it is particularly important to take control of the impact you have – as there is a multiplying effect that leaders' actions and behaviours have. A leader is always 'on stage', a role model, and people see what you do, so your ripple effect is a reality.

That is why we have written this book for you, to give you an opportunity to reflect on and build the impact you want and choose to have, in order to be the most successful leader you can be – for the benefit of those you work with, your organisation, its customers and partners and, of course, yourself! It can help you in interactions with your family and loved ones, too.

Everyone can have good, or even great, impact and, even though this book is written specifically for leaders, the dynamics of impact and many of the ideas in this book can benefit non-leaders and future leaders, too. Informal leaders often have strong impact; that is why they are leaders, even though they do not have a formal leadership role.

Leadership and impact are an art, not an exact science. There is not just one way of being a great leader. Being a great leader is not about cloning someone else. The most impactful leaders we have encountered authentically fine-tune their actions and behaviours to the situation they are in and the people they are with. No one gets it right all the time, but we can all maximise our impact with greater awareness of it and focus on it.

As leadership and impact are an art, we recommend that you view and use this book as a guide and a source of inspiration for impact-creation. You have your own unique way of being a leader and this book is here to give you food for thought and concrete practical ideas for impact at work that you can then start applying to your specific situations.

Whatever impact you want to achieve, we recommend you always do so from a win-win perspective – the impact should benefit everyone involved and, ideally, not just in the short term. And your impact should be in harmony with the organisational direction, vision and strategy.

Having worked with many hundreds of leaders, their teams and organisations all around the world for more than the last 20 years, we are intrigued and inspired by the concept of impact. We have experienced leaders with great, positive impact and those with less effective, and sometimes even very negative, impact. What makes the difference? We would argue that it starts with awareness – in two areas – self-awareness and social awareness. The more aware you are of yourself – your thoughts, feelings, values, stressors and energisers – and the more you are aware of the world around you, the more you can start to take control of your impact and start to shape the impact you want or need to have to be successful.

Awareness is a bit like a muscle in your body, it needs to be used, trained and flexed to build strength.

How well trained is your 'awareness muscle'?

Have you been training it lately? Or have you expected it to be in fine shape without any work? Could you do more to build its strength?

When was the last time someone knocked you with their rucksack while turning around in a cramped commuter train? Or seemed to ignore you in a meeting? Or were oblivious to the fact that they were holding up a whole aeroplane aisle of people while talking to their friend instead of getting into their seat? Or didn't remember you, even though you know you've met several times before?

In all those scenarios, their awareness muscle probably was not as well trained and engaged as it could have been. And the impact on you was probably not great, right?

A few years ago, there was a documentary/reality show on UK TV called *Boss Swap*. The idea behind the series was to have two leaders from two different companies swap places for two weeks. This was a very interesting 'social experiment' and we remember one episode in particular where the impact the leaders had in their new, temporary role was massively hindered by their lack of awareness of their new environment, not thinking through how different the reality of an estate agent from London and a used car salesman from Yorkshire is.

The point is that we all have an impact, even when we do not think we do, so do not leave your impact to chance. Start your impact strategy by becoming more aware.

How this book works

This book is divided into three parts and can be read from beginning to end or you can jump straight to the chapters that are most relevant to you. Regardless of which approach you take, we recommend at least reading Part 1 first.

Part 1 explores impact from a general perspective: what it is, why it is important and how it can be developed.

Part 2 explores impact in the context of different stakeholders and provides food for thought and practical ideas for how to achieve impact with some key stakeholder groups. Each chapter in Part 2 is structured like this:

- Self-assessment
- Exploring the stakeholder group
- A story of impact
- Solutions and tools
- Voice of impact (how impact feels and works)
- More solutions: the role your own thoughts, feelings and behaviours plays
- Summary
- Self-assessment

Part 3 explores impact in the context of specific desired outcomes and gives a step-by-step Roadmap, guiding you to insight for your specific outcomes. The chapters focus on four common examples of outcomes, but the Roadmap structure can be used for any outcome that is relevant for you. The steps in the Roadmap are:

1. Decide on the outcome
2. Set a target date
3. Understand the stakeholders
4. Assess the current reality
5. What do you and others need to learn
6. The Game Plan
7. How do you need to behave
8. Acknowledge obstacles
9. Communicate, communicate, communicate
10. Challenge the Roadmap
11. Measure the success

Throughout the book, we have created stories to describe how impact at work can look and feel and how it can be created. For those of you who have read our first book *The Team Formula: A Leadership Tale of a Team Who Found Their Way,* you will recognise the characters from that book in these stories.

Impact happens through knowledge and skill but, maybe, most importantly, through behaviours. If you want to achieve positive impact, pay particular attention to behaviours. How we behave and conduct ourselves has an impact on others, creating ripple effects that may go much further than we can imagine.

This is a practical book

This book applies to all levels of leaders, from CEOs all the way to junior frontline leaders, and many of the concepts discussed can be relevant and useful for non-leaders, too.

It is a practical book, so do not just read it, take action and choose to implement your solutions for positive, respectful, results-driven impact. You decide how much value to take from this book, you choose your impact.

Many of the ideas, solutions and tools that are listed in a given chapter can be equally valuable and relevant for another situation or another stakeholder group. So take a step back and reflect on your impact opportunities as a whole and find your own tailor-made approach to impact.

As impact is not an exact science, often there are not absolute answers. This book presents reflection point opportunities for your situation to trigger your thoughts for new ideas uniquely shaped by you. This book is here to give you food for thought as well as concrete practical ideas.

It is over to you. What impact are you choosing to have?

We wish you great leadership impact!

Part 1

Impact generally

What is impact and how do you get it?

The general concept of impact is explored in this first part, with reference to research on the subject.

What is impact?

Impact on – have a strong effect on someone or something.

Oxford Dictionaries

You always have an impact on people and the world around you, whether you pay attention to it or not. The strength and effectiveness of that impact can vary greatly. Ultimately, everyone is responsible for the impact they have and the impact they want to have. And the more senior you become as a leader, the more people you impact and, therefore, the more responsibility you have for making sure you get it right. That is how important your impact becomes.

To have impact is closely linked to the ability to influence. The difference between influence and impact, even if they overlap at times and it can be a question of semantics and interpretation, can be described like this – 'If you can influence you have an impact.' To influence someone is to make them take on board our ideas, suggestions or directions. This can happen through logic, facts, behaviours, emotions and peer pressure – to mention a few. When you have influenced someone to take on a new thought, argument, action or behaviour, you have had an impact on them.

It is *how* you do business that creates your impact

B2B: business to business.

B2C: business to consumer.

These are common ways of describing if a business is providing products and services to another business or directly to the consumer, the end user.

This is, to some degree, an important distinction as it impacts or even dictates how an organisation is organised and how it needs to operate.

But, ultimately, all business is H2H – it is *human to human*. It is *people* who make decisions to buy or not buy, to stay loyal to a brand or not, to recommend a company or not.

We may, for example, think that we have a contract with an *organisation* to deliver service, but that is only part of the truth – it will always be *people* who decide to sign that contract or not. If that person or those people do not have a great experience with us, they may choose to sign a new contract with someone else instead of signing or re-signing with us.

All of this may be more obvious in a B2C scenario, where a customer can vote with their feet and decide to not come back if the experience was not good.

But do not underestimate the power of the human aspect of *all* contacts an organisation and its people have. It is all about people. *People* make decisions. Connections happen between *humans.*

And this is why *how* we conduct business, *how* we behave in interaction with others, *how* we make others feel, is so important – and, if anything, is only becoming more and more important. Every interaction matters as well as the impact you have in each interaction. You are not just representing yourself, you are also representing the whole organisation and what it stands for.

It is the same within an organisation. No one is an island and, as you do not work in isolation, you need to constantly, continuously have an effect on people around you to achieve sustainable, long-term business results. In fact, throughout the history of mankind, the ability to create relationships with others, to connect and collaborate with others has been a key success factor. The concept and power of impact have always existed.

Impact starts from within

How you feel about yourself affects how you think about yourself, and how you think about yourself affects how you feel about yourself. Everything that goes on inside of you will, in some way, leak into the world around you. So the most important factor to consider when assessing your current impact or planning for your desired impact is how effectively you are leading yourself and taking control of your 'inner system of self'. This inner system consists of your beliefs about yourself, your self-esteem and level of self-confidence, driven by your thoughts and feelings. It is your whole mental and emotional self and a big driver of everything you do and what the world experiences with you. If you want to have a great impact on the world around, start first within. Get to know and understand yourself so well that you recognise and can take control of the impact you have. We will refer to various aspects of, and tools for, proactive self-leadership throughout the book.

Feeling inspired to inspire others

Recently, we travelled to Belgium where we were due to facilitate a self-leadership development programme that we have delivered many times before. We started the two days not feeling as good as we would want to feel to be truly effective. This was unusual for us. We were both tired and, as we had run this programme many times before, we realised that we needed to do something to make us feel different and reignite our own thoughts and feelings around what we were about to deliver.

Standing at the front of the big room, laid out with 20 chairs and a selection of round tables, we started to prepare the room for the days ahead of us. Elisabet turned to Mandy and said:

'How do we want to *be* today?'

'I think we need to be inspired so that we can be inspiring to others,' Mandy replied. 'I think that will affect the group really positively.'

Elisabet quickly added, 'We need to intentionally *be* inspired and, if *we are*, then this inspiration will leak into the group.'

'So, how can we change the way we feel?'

We brainstormed ideas to change that internal feeling and our internal dialogue. Moving from how we did not want the session to be, we started thinking and talking about times we had felt inspired while running this programme and how much we knew it had inspired others as well as us. We reflected on the many times when it had made a big difference to people. That started to inspire us again. We also brainstormed a few ideas of how we could create some additional exercises for the group, as we know that we are both greatly inspired by creative dialogue and action. We got excited remembering numerous stories people had shared with us regarding the progress they had made as a result of the programme. We played stories back to each other, which reenergised us and inspired us. We wanted that result again.

After the session, in the feedback process, almost everyone wrote the actual words that, in some way, they had felt *inspired.* We had not even uttered the word once, but the participants had experienced our heartfelt inspiration and it had been contagious. That was exactly the outcome we had hoped for and expected.

One of the key reminders for us here was that it was not about 'artificially' trying to inspire others from a state of non-inspiration ourselves. No, the key was first to be inspired ourselves, as, when we experience something ourselves, it is almost impossible not to create the same feeling in those around us. Good or bad. So our internal feeling does not just affect ourselves but also our external impact and the results we get.

Effective leadership impact comes down to this: *what state (of mind/emotion) do you want to elicit in others? Therefore, what state do you first need to elicit in yourself?*

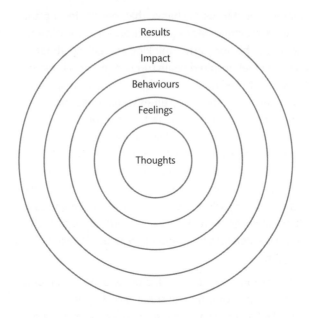

The (2020 Vision) Leader Impact Model™ This describes the ripple effect of leading and managing your inner self, which is illustrated in the figure above.

Your impact is about the ripple effect you create

Impact happens on a one-to-one basis, with individuals, and on a one-to-many basis, with teams and groups.

Negative impact may, for example, be as simple as checking emails on your phone when in a one-to-one situation. *How do you think that makes the other person feel? What impact are you having on them? Will they want to go that extra mile for you? And who are they meeting next? How may they affect that person as a result?*

Equally, if you are presenting to a room full of people, handing out awards and getting the recipients' names wrong, your personal brand will be negatively affected. People will feel that they are not important enough to be remembered or that you did not care enough to pay attention to the details. And people tend to remember those situations, so you will now have to work harder to reclaim some lost credibility and achieve the impact you want.

Positive impact can be as simple as saying thanks to someone who helped. It does not matter how small or large, just taking the time to stop and say thanks can have a huge impact on people. **In the busy world that we live in we can easily forget this important and impactful effort.**

A senior leader shared with us that he created this reaction in a team member whom he had sent an email to.

> *'It was a simple thank you email for my contribution to the team with some positive comments on developments and progress within a year. He made it personal to me and my situation, I felt very happy, pleased and proud. It made me more confident in my role which gave me more enthusiasm and energy.'*

It is a great example of that daily ripple effect we can have.

> **I've learned that people will forget what you said, people will forget what you did, but people will never forget how you made them feel.**
>
> Maya Angelou

Creating an impact strategy

Given that impact is very important, you need to challenge yourself to become aware of the impact you have or maybe lack. You may have a lot of strategies – for the business, for change initiatives, and more – but you also need to have a strategy for your impact and, therefore, what that will do for the business. What all leaders have in common is that they always operate through others; they need to enable employees to do a great job. This is why your impact becomes your most important strategy in order to deliver the desired and expected results.

Your impact is and should be bigger than you. And, as a senior leader in particular, it is not about raising your own profile; your focus on impact is for the good of the business, the greater good. Consistent and/or powerful impact creates your legacy, what the history books would say about you, what you become known for. Your legacy is also your personal brand. *What do you want to be known for? What legacy do you choose? When you move on to the next role, what do you want to be remembered for?*

Impact has always been important, but often more of a subconscious occurrence than a focused effort. The awareness of its importance has grown over time, hence also the need to, at a minimum, manage or, ideally, even create the impact you *want* to have rather than just accepting the impact you naturally have.

If you are a senior leader, your impact is also magnified. You set the pace for your organisation. You need to be intentional about your impact – you need to lead and role model the kind of impact behaviours the organisation, its people, its customers and all other stakeholders need.

Many people find the whole idea of creating impact challenging as it somehow seems false or conceited to them to *create* impact. They may, therefore, be reluctant to do something with this. This is particularly true for leaders in the early stages of their career. If you are a more senior leader, this concept should and needs to be at the forefront of your mind and something you should be comfortable with. This book is here to make you recognise that creating impact is a positive, powerful and respectful commitment to excellence – and it will tell you how to do it through specific, relevant, applicable solutions. And, most importantly, the book will also show you how to do it in an authentic way, a way that suits you.

Reputation and brand matter in all leadership positions and it is important for leaders to understand and work with that. Whatever leadership role you are in, it is your duty to ensure you have a strategy for your impact.

Things move fast; we are all surrounded by constant change. Leaders need to create impact in the moment, to not lose the power of that moment. No one is perfect and no one will get it right all the time, but they need to at least seize their most important moments and create the impact that will help them connect with others in a respectful way, to create trust, get others to listen to them, to influence effectively, and to drive results and everything else that comes with leading.

Going into the future, our ability to have a good or even great impact is becoming more and more important. We all need to think about the effect we have on others and what effect we want to have. 'How' we operate rather than simply 'what' we do is becoming more and more critical to success. It is all about how we impact people, the business and the world around us. In fact, it is fast becoming *the* differentiating factor for successful executives, leaders and organisations overall, something that we observe every day in our work.

And, considering that leaders are increasingly connected 24/7 through social media, you are always *on stage*, so the need to manage your impact is crucial. By actively *creating the impact* they want, leaders are demonstrating they are more in charge of, and can better predict, the outcomes they get. We all need to manage our personal impact and the effect our impact has on all our stakeholders, both in the short and the long term.

Leaders are often brought in to an organisation or are reassigned to a specific division or region to make a difference within a given timeframe. Some common examples of that are:

- A CEO is appointed to turn around a failing business;

- A CEO is appointed to lead the organisation through an aggressive growth strategy through mergers and acquisitions;

- A leader is asked to implement a specific change to how the organisation is working;

- An interim leader is asked to keep the organisation afloat while a new permanent leader is identified and hired.

Whatever the reasons are for the finite timeframe, any specific deadline brings about an extra need for putting an impact plan in place, where the leader asks her/himself: *How can I maximise my impact to deliver as expected within the timeframe?*

Whatever your impact ambition is, this book can help you build a tailored *impact strategy* for yourself. All the solutions in the book build on our five-step *impact strategy creator* below. Use it to start taking greater control of your impact by recognising the key areas in which you want to maximise your impact.

Five-step impact strategy creator

	Step	Reflect	Act
Step 1	Decide on the impact you want to have	What impact do you want to have and on whom?	List situations, initiatives, projects, places, teams, people, etc.
Step 2	Clarify what it will lead to	Why do you want to have that impact (what difference will it make)?	Map out the links between your impact and team/ divisional goals and organisational vision and mission, etc.

	Step	Reflect	Act
Step 3	Set target date	When do you want to achieve that impact?	Decide on milestones and deadlines, etc.
Step 4	Create an action/ behaviour plan	How will you achieve that impact?	List ideas for actions to take and behaviours to adopt. Consider the support you may need from others
Step 5	Decide on success measures	How will you measure/assess your impact going forward?	List possible measurements, such as surveys, feedback, productivity, etc.

Impact through position alone or through behaviour?

Stephen walked through the turnstiles for the first time since being appointed the new chief operating officer.

He was filled with energy and pride, having finally secured the senior position he had so coveted. This had been a long process, as all senior appointments are. He had waited for this day for six months. He had no history in the organisation and had been given a blank canvas for his role.

Sophia met him and showed him to his desk. *Desk?!* Stephen swivelled around, eyes darting to try to locate his office. *There wasn't one*, he realised. Before he could say anything, he was quickly whisked off to a meeting with the rest of the executive team, in an opaque glass-fronted conference room. His new career chapter started and, before he knew it, it was time for lunch and his first moment to reflect on his new reality.

➤

> *Why don't I have an office? How will this work? How will people know I'm senior? I need to show my authority and get myself an office!*
>
> Stephen did not get an office. The CEO had a firm policy that none of the executives would have an office, as Stephen realised when talking to a few of his peers. Stephen was surprised and initially perplexed and, ultimately, it forced him to think differently about his impact as COO. His impact would depend on his executive presence rather than the visual statement of power that comes with an office.

Someone who needs formal, external confirmations of power and position often can appear less senior and powerful than those who do not. The reason is that these external symbols are not a representation of real impact, only position and, if it looks like you need them, your ability to have impact may suffer. Sustainable, long-term impact comes down to behaviours, not symbols or what you have.

Sustainable, transformational change and impact happens at a behavioural level.

Taking responsibility for your impact

Whether he fully realises it or not, Stephen, in the preceding story, has a responsibility for his impact. Any leader has a responsibility to the people they lead: to add value to them, to be of service to them. In fact, the title CEO may well stand for chief *enabling* officer in addition to the more common chief executive officer and, if we extend that to all leaders, they are also in the business of enabling their employees and teams.

Yes, leaders have a responsibility to be intentional about their impact. And this is a great opportunity to make sure you are inspired and therefore inspiring, to truly feel good about what you do. Intentional, proactive impact increases your levels of success. It puts you in greater control of the outcome and it gets you there more quickly than the reactive learning over time would do.

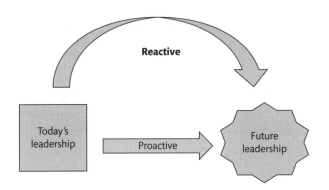

Understanding your audience

Every single person is different from the next and, therefore, needs to be approached differently. The Platinum Rule comes into play here – 'treat others as *they* want to be treated' - as opposed to the more commonly known Golden Rule – 'treat others as *you* want to be treated'. With the Platinum Rule, you do not assume that everyone is the same as you.

The Platinum Rule: treat others as *they* want to be treated.

Great communication, great influence and great impact always comes down to how well you understand your 'audience' and how well you adapt your style to match them. You are having your people/situation 'radar' on to tell you what is going on around you, what is coming up, what is around the corner, so that you can act and behave with integrity and presence and relevance.

Now, do not let that scare you, do not be daunted. You are not always going to get it right, but, with the intention, you are increasing your odds of greater impact. It is better to have some positive impact than none.

The Impact Meter in the following figure depicts how impact works. If you have a maximum negative impact, you are on −100, if you have no or neutral impact you are on 0, if you have maximum positive impact, you are on +100. You can check in on your Impact Meter daily or as a way to plan ahead for your week. Just like you would plan for *what* you are going to do, this is about *how* you are going to do it.

Imagine that your impact is currently 50 in a regular meeting with peers and you want it to be closer to 75 to have more influence over a decision. You may, for example, consider how to listen more intently to understand all the factors and how people are reacting. With that, you can then choose your approach and impact with greater precision. Even if your impact reaches only 60, it is still better than 50, and can be worked on from there for the next meeting.

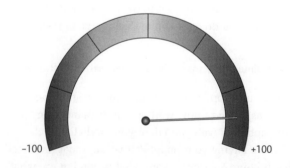

Impact Meter

To understand others also encapsulates being aware of and accepting differences. These differences can be down to aspects such as:

- personalities
- personal values
- age and gender
- local culture
- organisational culture
- knowledge
- background
- experience

Culture clash

Lindsay had recently arrived in the UK, taking up the role of senior vice president. This was her first role outside the USA, although she had been with the same organisation for eight years.

It was only a week in when she had her first opportunity to talk to the 200 employees in her department. Lindsay did what she had always done in these kinds of situations. She stood at the front, using her energy-infused rah-rah approach, as if trying to rally the troops into action.

It did not go down well. She missed the audience. Many instantly got the impression that she was not sincere, that it was just a put-on surface enthusiasm – some even felt as if they were being manipulated.

Lindsay herself was not specifically aware of her habits, therefore missing that her mannerisms were being interpreted completely differently from what she was used to. She was not familiar with local norms and habits and she had not thought about it being different, hence she had not done any

➤

research ahead of this event. She had thought of what she wanted to say, but not how she was going to do it.

She was also not picking up on cues for how others perceived her.

This resulted in making people suspicious. They thought she was a lightweight who was not in touch with reality and just too 'above it all'. It was not until one of her peers decided to enlighten her that the penny dropped and she could reflect on her approach going forward.

When people feel understood, when they have been acknowledged in some way, they connect more easily at a human level and have greater rapport. Rapport is when people feel connected, even though they may not even know why; it is just there. *When people are like each other, they like each other.* People being in sync with each other is, ultimately, what rapport is about. Without that synchronisation, that connection, your ability to influence others may be limited.

Think about it. If you are treated as if you are unique, as if you are understood, you are more likely to feel as if the person treating you in this unique way is having a positive impact on you. Right? So, to create the positive impact *you* want, you need to think about how you can treat others in a unique way, while still being authentic. Being authentic makes you feel comfortable and the effect is that it makes the other person at ease, too.

Being authentic and using your ULP

Just as every person is different from the next, so are you. You bring something that is unique and that differentiates you. You need to know what that is, so that you can tap into it and use it actively to bring out the best of you.

And that, in turn, brings out the best in others. Powerful impact is fuelled by your unique leadership points (ULPs), the combination of personality, background, experience, strengths and characteristics that you alone have. This is rarely fully understood, as most people do not have a comprehensive grasp of their strengths and what makes them unique. No one can be best at everything, but everyone is best at something. In Chapter 2 we will explore the use of ULP in more depth.

The best impact you can have is when you are 'being you'. It is good to be aware of when that works for you and when it does not. There are times when you need to adapt your style to connect with another person while still being authentic, to have an impact. So it is a fine balancing act between being attuned to yourself and others at the same time.

Leadership is not a science, it is an art form. It is the fine-tuning of behaviours that come from a combination of both self-awareness and social awareness.

How actions and behaviours drive impact

Our days at work are full of *what* we do and *how* we are. Our actions make up the *what* while our behaviours make up the *how*.

Work-life balance or not?

Christine wanted to encourage her team's work-life balance, so she kept telling her team members not to work too late, but instead go home at the end of the working day and spend time with friends, family and on hobbies. The team members were really pleased; they had a very positive reaction to this message and responded by leaving the office shortly after 5 pm on most days.

➤

> However, after about a week, they noticed that they had received late evening emails from Christine almost every day. This confused them, as her actions did not match what she was saying. *Why is she working late while telling us not to? She's clearly not meaning that we should go home at 5 pm. So what else is she meaning or not meaning? Can I trust her?*
>
> To top it all off, Christine decided to reward a couple of people who had been working all hours on a project, late at night and into the weekends. Now the team members were really confused.

Christine's action to promote better work–life balance made her employees feel valued and inspired and she got a good response from them. When she then did not behave in accordance with that, she was viewed with suspicion and it started to affect her credibility and the team's trust in her. By then rewarding the behaviours of working late, she exaggerated the negative impact. By not being consistent, she was having a negative impact on the team and was negatively impacting her own brand: how people perceived her. Inconsistency in actions and behaviours, low 'say-do ratio', swings the Impact Meter down.

This is what Christine could have done differently for more positive effective and powerful impact:

- Set an alarm to remind her to go home at a certain time.

- Not send emails too much out of office hours (even if she chose to write the emails then).

- Explain why she, on rare occasion, needed to stay later herself.

- Carefully think about what behaviours she rewarded in others.

▌ Reward people for working smarter, not longer.

▌ Reward linked to the results, with recommendation about how to work smarter rather than harder.

Having an impact is your job as a leader. It is not a nice thing to have, it is a necessity. It *is* the job.

Research on leadership impact

So where is the proof? Does leadership really matter that much? It sure does.

A study by Zenger and Folkman shows that leadership, whether good or bad, is contagious.[2] Of 51 leadership behaviours tested, the following 8 were the most contagious (in order of contagiousness):

1. Developing self and others
2. Technical skills
3. Strategy skills
4. Consideration and cooperation
5. Integrity and honesty
6. Global perspective
7. Decisiveness
8. Results focus

JR's contagious development

JR had always been curious; he enjoyed the whole process of learning and was always on the lookout for new things to explore or how to deepen his knowledge and enhance his skills in key areas of importance to him in his job.

This was impossible not to notice for people around him and, in fact, his team members were following a very similar

➤

pattern. JR certainly encouraged their development, but, most importantly, they could see that he also focused on his own.

The ongoing development meant that JR's trusted team members moved onwards and upwards at regular intervals. He did not mind, he was sorry to see them go but he also saw it as a natural result of their growth – of course they had to move on to greater roles.

Over time, JR took great pride in realising that not only had he supported his many team members to develop and grow, but they had also gone on and done the same thing in their new teams. The multiplication effect was so much greater than he could ever have imagined.

Leaders' behavioural habits clearly have an impact on their direct reports, who are also leaders *and* those leaders' direct reports. Further findings show that the most effective senior leaders have the highest performing direct report leaders.

A recent study by Hay Group concludes that up to 70 per cent of a team's climate is impacted by the leader and that 30 per cent of the difference in performance between teams is down to their working climate.[3] And business results show the next step of impact, where, for example, one company where leaders developed high-performing climates achieved 2.75 times the profit margin compared to those who did not.

Shaping the working climate

A sales team was made up of a number of very successful sales people. They all did well individually but there was not really any collaboration going on between them. There was the typical friendly, but competitive, culture often found in sales in particular. Their leader decided that he wanted them to change that. He decided to change the focus of their sales meetings. Instead of just talking forecast and numbers he wanted them to start opening up and sharing all their

> knowledge, experience and best practices with each other. Numbers could be done via email, he decided.
>
> The leader set the tone and stayed the course by not deviating from the collaborative and sharing focus. And the results started rolling in. The team stopped competing and started sharing. A new culture of trust started to take shape. And, within a year, they had *doubled* their sales.

Similarly, Gallup's research on Employee Engagement shows that team leaders 'account for at least 70% of the variance in employee engagement scores across business units'.[4] And Employee Engagement itself positively impacts the following nine performance outcomes:[5]

- customer ratings
- profitability
- productivity
- turnover (for high-turnover and low-turnover organisations)
- safety incidents
- shrinkage (theft)
- absenteeism
- patient safety incidents
- quality (defects)

The costly lack of engagement

A company's finance department had experienced internal conflict for quite some time, which had not been properly dealt with by any of the people involved. One of the accountants was so hurt and angry that she could not properly focus on her job. She was more engaged in her anger and looking at what her colleagues were doing or not doing, than she was in her own job.

➤

She started making mistakes in her job, which included not paying out customer credits on time, which, in turn, affected one of the biggest clients several times. Eventually, the client got tired of the bad treatment and removed their business from the company.

This backlash was a big wake-up call for the manager who had allowed conflicts to fester. She knew people did not enjoy working together but still had just put her head in the sand and hoped the problem would go away.

When she finally took action, the first thing she did was to sit down with each team member individually, talking to them, taking genuine interest in how they were finding their work and work situation. First, this was met with some hesitation, as it was not what they were used to, but, little by little, the team members began to open up and this gave the leader the insight she needed to continue to build engagement.

In every day, there are 1,440 minutes. That means we have 1,440 daily opportunities to make a positive impact.

Les Brown

The why and how of achieving impact

There are many reasons to focus on your impact. In fact, so many benefits exist. There are a few included in the following figure.

Impact happens in the moment

If you want to have greater impact, you have to be in the moment, be 100 per cent present, to make the people you are with feel that they have your full attention and that they matter the most. It is all about how you make people feel in that moment – they feel important, there is nowhere you would

rather be and, therefore, there is nowhere they would rather be. It also requires you to have a laser focus and not to multitask.

It is important to remove distractions, putting the phone away, not checking emails, staying focused. When you are in the moment, you will gain more from people. That moment that we just had has gone, the next moment is not here yet and the only thing we have is 'now', so create your impact in this moment.

Besides, studies show that people who multitask may reduce their productivity by as much as 40 per cent,[7] so focus is always a great idea.

Impact happens all the time, whether intentional or not.

The key to *effective* impact is, therefore, to be intentional about it, to decide 'this is the impact I want and choose to have'. Being intentional about it means you are choosing the effect you have on those around you and that gets you more sustainable results.

Positive impact can help you get your message across, make people feel inspired to act and drive better results. This fuels a strong positive impact spiral, where behaviours are contagious and the impact magnifies as it spirals upwards. Adversely, if you do not know what impact you have, your impact can be negative as our story 'Don't put your head in the sand' later in this chapter demonstrates.

When having a negative impact, you are achieving negative results, as you are impacting people in a negative way. And, if you are, for whatever reason, not able to have the impact you need, your results will suffer.

Blaming others and not taking responsibility for actions, behaviours and results creates a negative impact spiral. It makes other people fearful, reluctant to take responsibility, hence feeding a spiral of blame.

You are in control of that spiral and that spiral can spread to others. Others will then see that behaviour and think it is OK to behave like that. Behaviour breeds behaviour and that is how the spiral starts, in a positive or negative way.

Let us take a look at how you can achieve impact. More detailed information on how to achieve impact for specific audiences or a few key situations is given in the later chapters of this book.

Spreading the bad mood

Samuel was in a bad mood. His wife had really annoyed him this morning by being so negative about her new job. She seemed miserable and downbeat, and she was complaining that everything was wrong. Samuel had tried to help her see that it was not, but it had not done any good. He was frustrated with her being so despondent when she had no reason to be.

On his way into the office, he was reflecting on this and he was feeling pretty despondent himself. He walked into his office, head down, with a grumpy look on his face, and his shoulders were slumped. It was obvious he was not in a good place. One of his direct reports came towards his office and saw his demeanour. 'I am not going in there', she thought. Samuel barked an order for her to come in and discuss a report with him.

She came out of his office a while later feeling despondent; she swept out of his office ready to spread the word that Samuel was in a foul mood today.

1. What goes with the title?

We are all bigger than our title. If we have a title at work, it does not mean that is *all* that we are. Besides, with all these complex titles, who knows what the job really is? What is a head of strategy, senior independent non-executive director, CPO, COO, CMO, CIO? These roles vary so widely from one organisation to another. One thing that it does say is that your title has an impact, it has a set of expectations that go with it. If you are the CEO, then you had better behave like the CEO.

A title can carry impact, particularly in a traditional, hierarchical environment. It can be a door opener, but, unless it is supported by impactful behaviours, that impact may be short-lived. We can be an informal leader in the way we behave and not in title, that has just as much impact.

2. The way you behave and your habits

If you are in a room and the most senior person walks in, yet you have not met them, how do you know? How do you know they are the most senior person when they walk into the room? Should they bring their title in first? No, it is their actions and behaviours that differentiate them.

We are not what our title says. Yet, we can have a great impact by thinking of our title as something that represents us. What our title says sometimes can speak louder than what we say. If a senior leader comes to a meeting, the fact that they are attending can say enough before they have opened their mouth and said anything. There is an expectation that goes with the title. What would the meeting be like if they were in that meeting and what would it be like if they were not there? That tells you about the impact they have or are having.

There is an impact that is driven by your position and the kind of reach that you can have in that position. On many occasions, people do not think about their position as powerful, yet others around them do, so that in itself sets an expectation.

Recently, I was in a meeting where a team member constantly said, 'As a director, I think we need to do X? As a Director my role is X.' All it did was demonstrate how much they were *not* behaving like a director. If you have to say you are a director, then you are not. You need to behave like one.

3. Being a great communicator and listener

Think about your communication messages: 'What are you saying in your non-verbal communication?' Your impact has to take into consideration your appearance, physiology, voice and the words you use. Your words can be a representation of your inner world, your thoughts and feelings. Working with someone recently who kept describing the organisation as a battle field, this was creating a feeling of battle and conflict in the people around him. As a leader, you have a significant impact with your words.

4. ULPs – unique leadership points

We all have ULPs, our unique leadership points, and it is important that we are aware of them. Understanding our strengths and knowing them is as important, or more so, as knowing our developments. When we know our strengths and use them positively, they form our ULPs.

An engaging meeting

People noticed JR when he came into a room. It was his energy and enthusiasm that were particularly infectious. He had called his team together for a strategy planning session. As so often with his team, the room was buzzing with eager anticipation. These sessions were always good; they all knew that, so they came with that expectation. He was almost overwhelmingly positive.

He started the meeting with a story linked to their vision: how they would revolutionise the industry. His plans were ambitious, almost on the verge of unbelievable, but people always believed in his message. He had an uncanny ability to rally people around big dreams for the future. He could galvanise people to the degree that they really trusted they could do it – and they did.

Ahead of the meeting, JR had successfully pre-framed what they would talk about, which helped him, as usual, to make it a success. His pre-frame message held the same kind of energy and hope that would then be matched in the meeting itself. People came ready to engage.

JR was well known for rallying people, getting them to believe in what he was talking about. His passion was demonstrated because he really was behind his big vision and ambitions; he talked about ideas that were a long way into the future.

> JR always did this in a caring and empathetic way. He was full of smiles. He liked bringing people together with diverse backgrounds from different industries, countries and cultures. He felt it made for more creative and innovative thinking. JR had the ability to make you feel like you were the only person that mattered at that time and in that moment.

The results in the story were not a fluke, as JR was well aware of his strengths and knew from experience that these strengths worked as a lever for team commitment. He was also consistent in his behaviours so you always knew what you could expect from him.

Unique leadership points can create a great impact on others and are made up of a combination of the following components:

- expertise and experience
- personality
- strengths
- reputation/brand
- intelligence
- sense of quickness, urgency
- appearance and physiology
- presence
- making people feel seen and heard
- motivation

5. Leadership radar – being really aware

Do not put your head in the sand

What happened (Stephen's story)

It was time for the organisation to cut costs, again. This time, there was a real urgency to make an impact to the bottom

➤

line quickly. Stephen was being pushed hard to cut resources; that meant losing a large number of his people. It was August and he had to get the impact onto the bottom line by the end of the year, yes, the end of December. This was going to be tough in so many ways. Stephen knew what he had to do, but he really didn't like being told exactly how to do it. These were big numbers he was being asked to cut.

Stephen had to hunker down and get on with the job. He did not feel comfortable; of course he could do it, he had carried out this kind of procedure many times in his career, but this time it was different.

Stephen had asked both Lewis and JR to join him at this company, luring them from their last company with a great package and promise of an exciting job and career. He remembered being enthusiastic and keen during their interviews and he knew he could persuade them to come and work for him. After all, they had always enjoyed working for him previously and they trusted him. Stephen respected Lewis and JR and the feeling was mutual.

Now here he was having to tell them they were being given three months' notice and that they 'may' have a job at the end of it in the new reorganisation or they 'may not'. Stephen knew who was going to make it and who was not. He could not tell them, though. So he decided to avoid them, not to put himself in that difficult situation.

JR was going to definitely make it, Stephen would make sure that he came through the interview rounds with the new panel and get a job at the end of it. He started to avoid JR and Lewis; he made himself busy when they tried to talk to him and he disappeared whenever either of them wanted to connect. Stephen just made himself unavailable, he simply disappeared. He was sure that he could get through this without any form of confrontation. Stephen knew what was coming, Lewis and JR did not.

The Impact it had (JR's story)

I cannot believe that Stephen is avoiding me. I must have really upset him by something I have done in this new role. Maybe he thinks I cannot do my job. Maybe he is going to fire me because I have not lived up to his expectations. Stephen always did like the work I did in the last company, he was a walking ambassador for my work.

I just do not understand what I have done. I know he is upset with me because he is not being his normal energetic and enthusiastic self. He avoids eye contact and, last week, when I saw him in the corridor, he literally ran in the opposite direction. I am sure I am letting him down. I think I had better look for another job. I am feeling more convinced that he is going to get rid of me as part of the new cost cutting. I am not going to let that happen; I have a family to take care of so I am going to start looking seriously for a new position. He does not want me around and it is easy for him. I am last in and so I can be first out. I really think I have let him down in some way.

In this example, Stephen's behaviour has a huge impact on JR. JR starts to create stories about what is happening as there is a void, a lack of information. Of course, Stephen cannot give him all the information as it is a confidential and complex process, but the way he is behaving, which is very opposite to the way he normally behaves, allows JR to form the wrong conclusions and Stephen is about to lose the one person he wants to stay in the organisation. So, what was Stephen's impact and what else could he have done?

Stephen did not have his leadership radar engaged. His own emotions of fear and self-blame made him shut down and, therefore, unaware of his negative impact on JR.

To get a better result, he could have:

- ▌ faced the fear and got on with it
- ▌ planned for the ongoing communication that is always needed in times of change
- ▌ managed the informal communication: corridor chats and instant messaging
- ▌ reached out in some way, instead of withdrawing
- ▌ had a dialogue with JR and told him what he could tell him
- ▌ considered how his uncharacteristic behaviours might affect JR

JR could also have stepped up and approached Stephen and voiced his concerns, instead of making incorrect assumptions. In fact, this is true for any of us – whenever we find ourselves in that communication void, we can take responsibility for closing it rather than fuelling unsubstantiated doubts, hunches and rumours.

So what is a leadership radar? Well, just as a ship has a radar to detect what is going on around it, as a leader, you need to have your radar out to pick up what is happening in your inner world of self and outer world of people and environments. This can also be described as self-awareness and social awareness, which is at the core of emotional intelligence (EQ).

To switch on your internal leadership radar, you become aware of things like:

- ▌ how you feel
- ▌ what you are thinking
- ▌ your reactions
- ▌ what energises you
- ▌ what stresses you

▌ what your values are

▌ what motivates you

If you, for example, do not recognise that you are feeling stressed or frustrated, you will not be able to adjust your own behaviour to the situation you are in. If, on the other hand, you become more aware of what is going on inside you, you can take greater control of your state of mind and how that reflects outwards. You can take control of your own thoughts, feelings, actions and behaviours so that your impact on others is what you want it to be.

Do you want your impact to be inspiring, engaging, energising, thought-provoking, provocative, collaborative, enlightening, daring, different? Whatever impact you are going for, engage your inner world first.

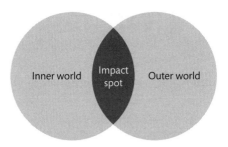

To switch on your external leadership radar, you need to observe, listen and explore the world around you to better understand the environment, situations, moods, interests and political/social landscape. This might mean getting to know people you are working with much better than you do now.

Effective system thinking, using your leadership radar

Once your radar is on, you need to understand the system you are in. When it comes to system thinking, usually, there are two main systems to consider, the internal system of the organisation and the external system, which is everything outside the organisation that touches it in some way. We would also add the 'inner system' of self (see Chapter 1). These three systems, when interlinked, show the complete picture of your ripple effect as a leader. By understanding each of them, you can consciously choose how to behave, act and communicate in order to influence and achieve the strategic aim of the organisation.

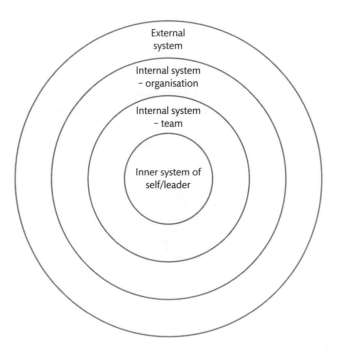

Being aware of your personal values

How do you feel when doing something or reacting to something? Chances are, if it feels good, you are doing something that is in line with your values.

And, if it does not, you are probably doing something that goes against your values.

Awareness of your values allows for better decisions and more conscious impact. If you know your values, you can tap into them more intentionally. Values are, for most people, both conscious and subconscious. You may be aware of some of them, but probably not all. What is good to think about, though, is that, whatever they are, they will drive your behaviours, and mainly in a subconscious way. This is why you absolutely need to know what they are so that you can judge how they create the results you get.

You will always act in line with your values, whether you know it or not. You have values for a reason, whether you know them or not. So they have an impact and effect on the way you behave. You can feel positive when working with your values or not positive when you are working against them. If you feel positive, then you will create that feeling and reaction in others too. If you feel negative, then you create that feeling in others. So, if you know your values and can work with them, you will take much more control of your impact.

You can be more impactful when acting in congruence with your values. Others see you as more authentic and, therefore, buy more into what you are saying – creating followership. When you act with your values, you are being very authentic. There is a calm and sense of powerful presence that comes from acting in alignment with your values. Other people can see that you are congruent, and your confidence shines through.

Personal values are powerful and the potential pitfall comes when having a value clash with someone else or when you are consciously or subconsciously disrespecting someone else's values. This can cause a negative impact, creating retaliation and revenge.

Values clash

Anna truly believed that people should be treated with respect. She did not think that Samuel had just done that when he shouted at her team member, Christine, across the ➤

hallway. Samuel was calling out from his office across the entire open-plan office to ask for some financial reports that he wanted right now. And, from his tone, it was very clear that he meant 'right now'. His voice was highly pitched, angry, with a bark to it. Everyone could hear it. The whole department was almost holding its breath waiting for the response.

Christine very calmly picked up her laptop and took it into Samuel's office. Anna could feel the rage inside her, how dare Samuel speak to people in that way. It was outrageous and she was not going to let it happen. Now Anna was filled with frustration and was on her way to Samuel's office. Before she could stop herself, she had closed the door. She had to tell him the impact he had just had on her and the many people around them. And also how fast that message would get communicated to others around the business. It was not acceptable to Anna so she wanted Samuel to be aware of the impact he had. Samuel explained that he simply wanted a quick reaction and was keen and driven to achieve a fast result at that moment; he was being put under pressure from his boss, Stephen, and he tried to explain to Anna how it was not his intention to upset her or, indeed, anyone else. He had just been trying to get a fast result.

In this example, Anna had strong values of treating others with respect and dignity. Her values prompted a reaction from her to behave in a way aligned to her values – she did it in a respectful way herself. Samuel's values of being direct, driven and acting with a sense of urgency wanting to deliver fast results had a different impact on Anna and was not what he had intended. He had good intentions behind his values, but Anna did not experience it that way.

Just because values are not aligned does not mean you cannot have impact. What you need to do is respect others' values and find some common ground, a shared reason or outcome, where the other party feels respected and heard.

It is better to have an impact through respect and people feeling seen and heard, than to have impact through fear where people feel forced or coerced to do something. The first kind is self-generating and lasting, whereas the latter does not build commitment, loyalty, trust or longevity – people will not go that extra mile for you.

THE EFFECT ON CULTURE

Culture is a hot word in organisations. Everyone talks about it, many want to change the culture but find it is about as easy as finding a needle in haystack. This is because culture cannot be captured in processes, policies and procedures. Culture can be aided by a sensible infrastructure, but is, ultimately, shaped by people's behaviours and nothing else.

There is always a culture, wherever you work (just like any society is guided by its cultural norms) and the culture can either be left to its own devices or it can be consciously created, adjusted, tweaked or changed. You decide.

Transformational change happens at a behavioural level

So what is culture?

Culture simply determines 'how things get done around here'. It is usually implicit rather than explicit. It is not the 'what', it is the 'how' of business. It is how people react, behave and interact every minute of every day. It is not determined by a framed poster on the wall in reception, it is more complex than that. And this is the challenge with culture; the concept is simple but the implementation

➤

can be very complex as habits die hard and to change behaviours takes time. The leaders and their impact have a huge part in shaping this.

So where does culture start?

Leaders at all levels have a responsibility when it comes to the organisation's culture, but the buck stops with the CEO and the senior leadership team. Everyone's behaviours shape the culture, but the behaviours that are displayed by and accepted or even rewarded by leaders are the biggest culture shapers. They impact the culture the most.

The 'bad' culture shaper

Imagine a CEO who speaks about the value of transparency and openness, but who goes behind his executives' backs, sharing certain things only with his 'trusted few'. The executives that experience this become cautious, thinking it is not about transparency at all – I'd better tread carefully around here from now on. These executives, in turn, become less transparent with their teams, who become disenchanted by the false behaviours (not in line with the values) of their leaders. *That is how leaders shape culture.*

The 'good' culture shaper

Imagine a company that says it values and respects people's work–life balance. The leaders then reward and praise people who work smarter and within work hours, and work together in teams to achieve. They are rewarding what they value not what they do not value (they are *not* rewarding people who work long hours and sacrifice their personal lives). *That is how leaders shape culture.*

Culture should be on every board's, executive team's and leader's agenda. Leaders at all levels set the tone for 'how things get done'. Culture starts at the top, but cannot just be dictated from the top. It needs to resonate with people at all levels as something they would 'stand for' themselves.

So leaders who want to maximise the power that is culture must look to themselves first: How am I behaving? What messages am I sending through my behaviours? What behaviours am I creating in others? And then start changing and adapting their behaviours, creating new habits, if needed, to create the desired culture.

In a clear, strong, healthy culture, people know *exactly* how to operate and this helps them to act with integrity for the good of all constituents. This is the only way to long-term success.

Culture is *not* soft and fluffy – it is the strongest driving force of an organisation. How you behave as a leader and what behaviours you accept in others become the culture – make sure you are consistent by role modelling and rewarding the right behaviours. Leaders impact culture, full stop.

We have added 'The effect on culture, to the end of each of our chapters to keep the focus on your cultural impact.

There's no greater gift than thinking that you had some impact on the world, for the better.

Gloria Steinem

2

Impact on different audiences/stakeholders

Different people/stakeholders and the relationship the leader has with them require different considerations when it comes to impact. In this part of the book, stories paint the picture of opportunities for impact relevant to each different group.

Each chapter starts off by exploring that particular group of stakeholders, their needs and interests and how to take all that into consideration when deciding to have a greater impact on them. Short stories are used to illustrate opportunities and solutions for impact.

Impact on employees

Self-assessment

Before reading this chapter, do the following quick self-assessment.

How would you rate your ability to create impact on employees in these areas?

	1 Very poor	2 Poor	3 Just OK	4 Good	5 Excellent
Communicating and following through on vision with passion					
Treating people individually and valuing differences					
Getting teams to believe in themselves					
Being authentic at work which creates more positive results					
Managing your brand and reputation					

Exploring the stakeholder group: understanding your impact on employees

Let us start off with a cliché: *Employees are an organisation's greatest asset.* We cringed when we wrote that – did you cringe when you read it? It has probably been overused as a statement for decades, while not truly given the weight it deserves for the strategic importance it actually has in organisational sustainability and dependable financial results.

So let us unpack that statement and do it justice.

Why are employees so important?

Employees are hired to carry out the organisation's purpose. That purpose unites employees in providing a service, product or experience that is of benefit to the end user, such as a customer or patient. Each employee is recruited for their particular strengths, skills, competencies, experience, attitude and cultural fit.

When we are talking about attitude, we mean how a person looks at their job and how that attitude will affect the dynamics of the workplace. Cultural fit can mean the internal culture of the organisation or the culture of the geographical area you operate in. Understanding the cultural nuances will help employees navigate that particular environment. So, if you are in an innovative, fast-moving start-up environment, for example, employees must match and enjoy that pace and get energised by trying something new and being OK with the constant trial, adjustment and change that are part of the daily reality of start-ups.

What employees do, how they operate and how they behave, and what experience they ultimately create for the customer reflect back on the company. Every employee is a brand ambassador and needs to see themself as that *and* be seen as that.

Most organisations look for growth, greater productivity, more efficient use of resources and/or innovative solutions. In order to achieve that, they need to get their employees to effectively contribute to this by bringing their unique offering to work every day. It is then through collaboration with others that each person's contribution can come to full fruition.

When you look at all of this, you realise why your impact as a leader is crucial to getting the most out of your employees, so they can deliver the results the organisation depends on for its short- and long-term results.

What do employees need?

A global employee survey (by CEO/Gartner)[8] asked employees to rank their most important factors when choosing an employer. The consolidated results show that in the UK, for example, those factors were (in order of importance):

▌ work–life balance

▌ stability

▌ location

▌ respect

▌ future career opportunities

▌ compensation

▌ recognition

▌ people management

▌ development opportunity

▌ vacation

These factors can, of course, vary from country to country, based on the relevant current work situation. This is why it is so important to understand what employees value and need in order to meet those needs as well as possible. However, the list above gives a good indication of factors that matter to people at work, regardless of where they are based, although the order of these may vary.

Interestingly, the survey also shows that, globally, employees tend to stay longer in their jobs but are not necessarily

willing to go above and beyond what is expected of them –
clearly showing that employee engagement can be improved.

This brings us to the subject of employee engagement.
According to the world's largest study on employee
engagement, by Gallup, there are 12 key factors of
engagement. Employee engagement is beneficial not just to
the individual (to engage with your work is more enjoyable
and rewarding) but to the organisation. And, when you
look closer at those factors, you notice that the immediate
manager has an impact on most, if not all, of those
factors.[9]

Individually, employees may have other needs and
expectations, which can be assessed and understood only by
leaders being aware of that, hence taking a genuine interest
in people. That is how they can treat each person most
fairly and effectively and, therefore, get the best out of each
person.

A story of impact: the award ceremony

It was the annual January kick-off conference. A total of 556
people were gathered in Frankfurt for this global get-together.
Anticipation was high. The new leader, Stephen, was about to
go on stage to hold his opening address and then, later on,
present the high-performance awards for the previous year.

Stephen felt rushed. He had been busy on budget reviews,
along with all the challenges that come with the necessity of
moving house for his new position, for the last few weeks. He
had not taken the time to focus much on this event. It just
had not been a priority.

He had spent time preparing his keynote speech; he had
been thinking about what to say and how – he had mentally
been rehearsing that.

➤

The award ceremony, on the other hand, had not taken up any of his time. It was not needed, he was just going to read out some names. Or so he thought.

Stephen was invited up onto the stage by the moderator to thundering applause. People had not seen him in action yet, but they had heard good things about him and were looking forward to hearing him talk.

Stephen's tall posture, with head held high and shoulders back, signalled confidence. He held his arms out in a welcoming gesture. His voice was crisp and clear as he scanned the auditorium. He was enthusiastic and he was instilling that in others.

'I've spent my first couple of months getting to know more about the business, and I like what I see. It's probably more impressive now I'm here and can see it from inside the organisation. I'm excited about what I see ahead of us.'

People in the audience were nodding, seeming to relate to what Stephen was saying. Stephen relaxed more and more as his talk progressed. Things were going well. His speech came to an end and the audience were listening intently, some of them were even on the edge of their seats.

Later in the day, it was time for Stephen to take to the stage again, this time in the capacity of senior-leader-who-gives-out-awards. The host invited Stephen to announce the first award winner, along with the reasons why they had been given the award. Stephen cleared his throat and spoke into the microphone:

'The award for Account Manager of the Year goes to a person who has shown outstanding attention to customer needs and who has created innovative solutions to customer challenges – while collaborating with numerous departments to deliver the results.'

Stephen looked up from the card he was reading. He was clearly reading a scripted message talking about a person to whom he was not relating.

'I am delighted to present this award to Mary Johnson.'

There was confusion in the room, with sharp intakes of air from a lot of people as they looked around at each other. There was no account manager called Mary Johnson. There was, however, a very well-known one called Maria Johnston. It was obvious that must be who he meant.

The host politely corrected Stephen by inviting Maria Johnston to come and get her award. Maria hesitantly got to her feet, looking embarrassed; it did not feel like a celebration, almost like it was not her award. Her colleagues cheered her on, but there was tension in the air. By the time she got to the stage, the applause was getting louder with a few whistles and shouts of support.

Most of this was missed by Stephen, as he continued the award ceremony and managed to mispronounce another couple of names before it was all over. His impact had started off well but finished somewhere completely different.

One of the hottest subjects at the evening drinks reception, when Stephen was not around, was about the errors at the awards.

I can't believe that Stephen got that so wrong, how come he didn't pay attention to their names? It is so important. If that was me and he got my name wrong, I would have felt really undervalued. He made it obvious he didn't care about the awards. I would have said something.

Does he not realise the impact of that? I had such high hopes for him but I am not sure any more. He started off well but now I don't know what to think.

I had a call with my team back at the office who are not even at the conference and even they asked me about it. News travels fast. Not a good first impression.

➤

Stephen started off well in this story. His preparation and presence during the opening remarks were strong, engaged and genuine – he made a good impression. Sadly, the impact of what happened later wiped out a lot of the credibility he had gained at the start.

There were a few issues at play here. Stephen had not prepared, it was just an award ceremony for him, not something he considered needed any work.

He did not pay attention because he did not take a genuine interest, and he was just rushing through it, reading words off a piece of paper rather than connecting with the people and their accomplishments. He also was not paying attention to people's reactions, because he did it again and again.

He had an opportunity to impact many people in that moment, and he missed it. So now it will take him a lot of time to regain that initial connection and start creating trust. Impression and reputation matter; they are vehicles of impact.

Solutions and tools

Here are some practical solutions and tools for having a positive impact on employees.

1. Have a vision and carry it through

There is something enormously powerful about a vision for the future. Just think of Martin Luther King Jr's famous 'I have a dream' speech, full of engaging description of his vision for a fair and equal world.

Visions that are communicated with passion and authenticity, and that give hope and a desire for action, can give great leverage for change and engagement at work.

Maybe it is your own vision or the established vision of the organisation that you are truly passionate about. Regardless, make it yours and embody it in everything you do. Find your own inspiration in it and then show it to the world. Make people *see* and experience you living it, not just talking about it.

Constantly make links to the vision, and help others connect the dots from what they are doing every day to the vision itself. Show them the way; that *is* the role of a leader. It is not an additional job or a nice thing to have, **it *is* the job**.

Use the vision as a guiding direction for strategies, tactical plans and communication. Show the link between initiatives, projects, actions and processes back to the vision. Make a point that everything is done for a reason.

Recognise when other people contribute to the vision too.

Martin Luther King Jr did not say 'I have a strategic plan'! It probably would not have been as compelling, would it?

Follow these steps to connect with and populate the vision:

▌ **Identify the vision** (the company's or yours) and write it down in a concise sentence – the shorter the better.

▌ **Explore it for yourself** so that you can fully relate to it, connect with it and be able to communicate it with authentic passion and commitment. Think through what the ambition of it will achieve and how people may be able to relate to it.

▌ **Refer to the vision** at regular intervals when communicating with employees, both in writing and in presentations and conversations. Make sure you link strategies and activities to the vision (clarifying *why* something is done), while also showing how strategies and activities have contributed to the vision.

▌**Formally recognise and even reward employees** whose actions and behaviours are in line with the vision and contribute to it. Consider introducing specific 'Making Vision Reality' awards where efforts with tangible outcomes are recorded. For example: 'This award is given to Lisa for consistently delivering on time, honouring our commitment to be the most reliable partner around.'

2. **Treat people as individuals and value differences**

See people for who they are. Really see them. Value each individual person for who he or she is. Being seen and heard tends to make people feel important and valued, and that creates a very positive impact where they want to put more effort in, stay more loyal, and give more of their thoughts and ideas.

Think of a time when someone really listened to you and valued your input. *How did you feel? How did you start to behave and what difference did it make to you, then the way you work and the way you interact with others and the impact on the bottom line?* In a world where there is so much change accelerated by digital transformation, we need differences to allow us to think of as many ways as possible. This is why we must appreciate difference as leaders. People will also work smarter if they are acknowledged and invited to bring their unique contribution in this way.

Here are some tips to get you started:

▌**Put together a set of questions** that you can use whenever you talk with an employee, in order to better understand them, their interests, their strengths and their unique contribution to the organisation. For example: *What are you working on right now? What strengths do you think you bring to the team? What opportunities do you think we should be focusing on as an organisation? If you could change one thing about what we do, what would that be?*

▊ **Use softening phrases** at the beginning of your questions. When asking questions, it can come across like a bit of an interrogation unless you use softening phrases. Using too many of them, though, is not recommended, as it can make you look too vague or, sometimes, even unsure of yourself.

Here are some examples of possible softening phrases in the context of asking questions: *I'm curious . . . I'm wondering . . . I was thinking . . . I was wondering . . . That's interesting . . . That's interesting, could you tell me some more? Tell me more . . .*

▊ **Think about the benefits of diversity in employees.** Ask yourself: *How can we achieve more through people having different origins, backgrounds, experience, interests and strengths? How can it help us drive continuous innovation and future success?* Then use the answer from those questions to guide you in seeking out and valuing diversity.

▊ **Communicate your commitment to and appreciation of diversity**. Notice when differences have delivered more thorough analysis, better decisions and more efficient solutions. Communicate that and encourage more of it to happen.

3. **Get teams to believe in themselves**

Just like an individual, a team can have varying levels of self-esteem.

When a team enjoys working together, is able to do a good job and its members are seen as important, the team will feel good about itself – it will have high team self-esteem.

Building team self-esteem is a way of increasing engagement in a team and it is done through role modelling of personal 'response-ability', clarity of purpose, performance feedback, development discussions, innovative ways of doing the job, genuine interest, celebrating success and making it contagious.

You have to put focus on the team self-esteem. Spend time on it, discuss and work out the following as a team:

▌ *What is our self-esteem currently like as a team? How much do we believe in ourselves? Do we take enough pride in what we do? What results have we achieved and how has that contributed to the organisation's success?*

▌ *What do we want it to be? (If different from what it currently is.)*

▌ *If there is a gap, how do we close the gap as a team? How can we build our genuine belief in ourselves? What are the proofs of what we are; what we have achieved and what else we can achieve going forward?*

4. **Be authentic, take off your corporate cloak**

The real Sophia

Sophia was told by her boss that she had not done well the previous week when presenting to the senior leader from New York. He was really harsh with Sophia. He told her that she seemed rigid and too prescriptive with her slides, sounding like she held a scripted monologue. She was not engaging in her way of speaking and others could not follow what she was saying. Sophia was talking about a complex subject and she had lost her audience. It felt too rehearsed, she was not open to questions and not open to hearing others' views. Sophia was shocked at this feedback, this was not at all how she normally was.

Sophia was passionate, she had a powerful message to deliver and was incredibly friendly and personable with people. In this presentation, however, she had been just too corporate and not herself at all. She was annoyed and, after talking to her coach, she worked out that she needed to take off her corporate cloak and be more herself. Be more passionate, talk openly and express herself, talk without her slides and talk from the heart. She decided to bring in more structure, but for her, not for the slides! She needed to forget that conditioning that she seemed to have picked up. She had one more chance to present this week and it had to be different. Sophia took off her cloak, let herself out and got great results which resulted in much better feedback! It was so much better; not perfect, but definitely better!

This story makes us wonder just how many of us feel like we are trying to be the perfect corporate citizen. We have so much training and conditioning to mould us into the way others want us to be rather than how we, individually, can be when we are at our best.

We are sometimes made to believe that we have to be:

- like others
- like our colleagues
- like the corporate person
- like our bosses
- like our peers
- like the competition
- like the perfect presenter, leader, boss, partner, etc

. . . when we really just need to be ourselves. When we are our authentic self, being ourselves, we are then showing others the best version of us.

In our work with senior leaders, people often wonder: 'Do you have to work on their areas for development, do you have to focus on what they need to improve in?' No is the answer most of the time we help them to be who they really are, bringing out the real person. If we are not careful with all that conditioning, we can become something we are not.

> **With all that conditioning we can become something we are not.**

That is not to say that we cannot learn and grow and change. Of course we can. The most powerful leaders, and the ones whose careers go the furthest, are those who are aware of themselves, being comfortable with who they are. They know when that works for them and, when it does not, they are able to adapt and change.

So take off your corporate cloak and bring out the real you, show that to others, make the most of it, connect with others through your authentic core and watch your career grow. There is only one you, make that count.

A few tangible ways for taking off that corporate cloak:

▌ **Become a great self-leader.** Get to know yourself by identifying your own values and passions, stressors and energisers. Write them down, together with any other information about who you really are as a person.

▌ **Figure out what your strengths are.** This can be done in a number of ways: observe yourself, ask for feedback, do a strengths assessment (e.g. StrengthScope). Examples of strengths could be: collaboration, results focus, critical thinking, creativity and empathy.

▌ **Think about how you can best use your strengths and characteristics at work.** Map out your responsibilities and tasks and match your strengths and characteristics to them, consciously thinking about how you can make the most of who you are and make that work for you. Fill in the table below.

Responsibility/ task	Strengths/ characteristics	How strength/ characteristics can best be used	How it will make a difference to the results

▌ **Observe the people you work with and note what their strengths and characteristics are.** This is a great reminder that no one is best at everything, but that everyone has a unique set of strong points and that there is not just one way of being a great leader.

5. **Be intentional about your brand and reputation**

How aware are you of your brand? Everyone has a personal brand and, therefore, a professional reputation.

In general, you could say that a brand is a concept, an expectation, that lives in the head of the customer. As such, the brand is made up of the product itself, the service that surrounds it and the communication about it.

When all these things are added together, an experience is created, a promise of what the customer can expect, which can be called a brand promise. And, as a leader, you have both a brand and a brand promise.

> **Your brand is made up by your unique strengths, expertise as well as your actions and behaviours.**

So what does *your* brand promise? What do people expect you to deliver? What previous experience have they had with you? Will they expect you to be dependable, creative or optimistic, for example? What is *your* brand all about? What words describe you?

Just like an organisation thinks about its brand, you need to do the same as a leader. Take control of your leadership brand to optimise your impact and aid your career. If you have not yet spent much time on this, here are some questions to start you working on it:

Start thinking of yourself as a brand

1. What do you wish for people to associate with you when they think of your name? What do you want to be known for? What will be your leadership legacy?

2. How will you make sure that people know that? How will you show it?

3. Is there a certain subject matter in which you want to be perceived as an expert or are there general qualities you want linked to your brand?
(Once you understand how you wish your brand to be perceived, you can start to be much more strategic about your personal brand. This does not mean you cannot be human.)

4. What is your 'superpower'? What do you do better than anyone else?

Start thinking of yourself as a brand
5. What do people frequently compliment you on or praise you for? What do other people see/experience when they meet you? If you do not know, ask for feedforward (feedback that drives you forward).
6. What is it that you bring to others? What are your strengths? When/how/where do you add value to others/ the organisation, etc? What is it that your manager, employees, colleagues, friends and clients come to you for?
7. What energises or ignites you? What are your true passions?

Carefully reflect on your personal and leadership brand at regular intervals. Make sure you know what your brand promise is. Act and behave consistently with that promise. You may find it helpful to create your own tagline and to keep this in your mind at all times to really *live* that promise. For example: *I'm a creative, open-minded leader. I'm a dependable, inclusive leader. I'm an empathetic and driven leader. I'm a strategic and innovative leader.* Act as if you are already there, as this is a great enabler to create the mindset you are after and the subsequent actions and behaviours.

Another consideration is whether you need to respectfully promote yourself, your brand. Typically, this is needed if your capabilities are currently unknown or you have a limited network. Keep in mind that self-promotion works really well only if it is done from a point of 'the value I bring to others' rather than enhancing yourself for the benefit of you.

Think about your brand like this: whether you choose to pay attention to it or not, you have a brand and a reputation. You will have much greater and more positive impact if you take control of it and decide what you want to be known for – and then act and behave accordingly.

There is only one you – make your impact powerful through a strong, authentic and win–win-focused brand and reputation.

Voice of impact

Impact is the feeling and response we create in others.

Here are some examples linked to this chapter of how an action or behaviour impacts people's feelings and, therefore, how they respond at work. This is how impact sounds and feels. They clearly show that what we do has consequences, good or bad. This gives us a greater understanding that we have the ability to affect our outcomes every moment of every day. This is a big responsibility and, as a leader, it is magnified through the wide sphere of influence that comes with a leadership role.

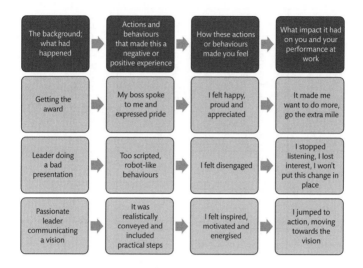

The background; what had happened	Actions and behaviours that made this a negative or positive experience	How these actions or behaviours made you feel	What impact it had on you and your performance at work
Getting the award	My boss spoke to me and expressed pride	I felt happy, proud and appreciated	It made me want to do more, go the extra mile
Leader doing a bad presentation	Too scripted, robot-like behaviours	I felt disengaged	I stopped listening, I lost interest, I won't put this change in place
Passionate leader communicating a vision	It was realistically conveyed and included practical steps	I felt inspired, motivated and energised	I jumped to action, moving towards the vision

More solutions: the role your own thoughts, feelings and behaviours play

When wanting to take control over your impact on employees, you first need to impact yourself.

> **What we think affects how we feel, and how we feel affects how we think.**

You can actively replace thoughts and feelings that are counterproductive to positive impact.

It is estimated[10] that a person experiences up to as many as 70,000 thoughts per day.

Many of those thoughts are habits that affect a person's mindset or outlook and, therefore, the impact they have on the world around them. It starts from within.

On the next page are some examples of negative thoughts, their impact on feelings and how they can be changed to new constructive thoughts to drive more effective impact behaviour.

Negative thought	Negative feeling	Ineffective behaviour	Constructive thought	Constructive feeling	Effective behaviour
This award ceremony is not so important	Apathy, lack of energy	Complacent, non-engaged communication	This award ceremony makes a real difference to people	Sense of importance, energy	Engaging and caring acknowledgement of employee's accomplishment
Why don't they get the vision? I've told them before!	Impatience, frustration	Get irritated with others when they ask for clarity around the vision again	I clearly need to communicate this vision more/differently as people are not yet on board – how can I make this more creative?	Curious and creative	Think carefully about how I position the vision with people in mind
I can't be myself at work	Feel constrained, incongruent	Behave impersonally and without passion	I'm able to be myself at work. People want to see the real person	Feel comfortable and at ease	I can talk openly and express myself. I can be passionate

Summary

Whether you are the CEO or a team leader, you get the work done through your trusted employees. You depend on them, and they depend on you to provide the leadership that makes it possible for them to do a great job.

Think of yourself as a great conductor of a philharmonic orchestra. By focusing on the impact you have on the orchestra (your employees), you are enabling them to perform for the benefit of the audience (customers and other stakeholders). You are enabling them to have a great impact on the audience. They deliver, you support.

Carefully think through what impact you want to have on them, how you want to make them feel. Focus on giving them that and let them get on with it. Your impact on employees is a big part of what your leadership needs to be about.

THE EFFECT ON CULTURE

As a leader, you are responsible for co-creating the culture; it goes with the territory of being a leader. Culture is 'the way things get done around here' and that starts with you. It happens minute by minute, leader by leader. Whatever you role model to employees will become the culture in your team and, therefore, also shape the organisation's culture. You are shaping it in every interaction and every behaviour you display. Now that is a big responsibility, so be wise about it. What culture are you creating in your employees? What's your impact? It starts with you.

Self-assessment

After you have implemented the solutions in this chapter, answer these questions again to see the progress you have made.

How would you rate your ability to create impact on employees in these areas?

	1 Very poor	2 Poor	3 Just OK	4 Good	5 Excellent
Communicating and following through on vision with passion					
Treating people individually and valuing differences					
Getting teams to believe in themselves					
Being authentic at work which creates more positive results					
Managing your brand and reputation					

Leadership is about making others better as a result of your presence and making sure that impact lasts in your absence.

Sheryl Sandberg

4
Impact on people more senior than you

Self-assessment

Before reading this chapter, do the following quick self-assessment.

How would you rate your ability to create impact on people who are more senior than you in these areas?

	1 Very poor	2 Poor	3 Just OK	4 Good	5 Excellent
Putting yourself in the shoes of stakeholders at a more senior level					
Asking smart questions as well as giving answers					
Being a mentor to others and learning from it yourself					
Behaving as if you are more senior					
Preparing for meetings on how you want to 'to be' not what you want 'to do'					

Exploring the stakeholder group: understanding your impact on people more senior than you

People more senior than you can be the person you report to, your CEO or anyone in between. It could also be someone in your organisation that you do not have a direct relationship with but who exists in your matrix. Seniority can also be down to tenure and experience.

These people can have positional power through the role that they have. As such, they can influence your career, by doing something as simple as talking to other senior

Christine's visibility

'I think Christine can do so much more than she's currently doing. I saw her drive some really creative conversations in the last team meeting.'

'I agree. I've also been very impressed with her. She jumped in to help out my team recently even though she didn't have to. Not only was she helpful, she added something we didn't have by offering a new and different approach to it. She was open and shared a lot with the team. We need that to happen much more around here.'

A number of other leaders around the table chipped in to share how they had experienced something similar. It became clear that Christine had made an impact on this senior team and that, in conversation, they all recognised and agreed she could, and should, take on a bigger role and contribution to the organisation.

leaders about who could get the next available job, for example. Typical career progression and succession planning conversations can go something like this:

What this interaction shows is how your actions and behaviours are noticed by senior leaders, whether you think about it or not. It is up to you to make sure they are aware of you, that you have impacted them effectively. They need to have you on their radar if they are an important stakeholder to you.

Do not get too caught up in thoughts about seniority so much that it affects the way that you behave and therefore makes you appear inauthentic. At the end of the day, they are also just people, and people connect with people. Be yourself, while understanding that you have the ability to influence people who are more senior to you, just as much as you can influence people who work with you (peers) or those who work for you.

In order to have an impact on senior people, you need to 'put yourself in their shoes', think in patterns similar to theirs (e.g. more strategically). It is important not only to use more senior thinking patterns but also to behave as if you are at the next level. If you behave in that way, then people will start to see your behaviour and start to see you operating at a more senior level than you are today. You need to 'behave as if' you are in the job. Ask yourself: *if you were them, how would you behave, what would you do?*

Why do you need to influence people more senior than you?

Senior people can influence more people than you can, either formally or informally due to their network and reach. They could help you in the future. They could introduce you to people they know. They could be vocal supporters for you. They can become your walking 'ambassadors', doing the work of talking about you to others for you. How many 'ambassadors' do you have? They can play an influential role in your career.

This is why you want to think carefully about the impact you currently have and the one you want to have, if not the same.

Imagine that you have a fully booked day where you are going from meeting to meeting. *What impact are you taking with you from one meeting to the next? What if you have a disagreement with your boss or a peer in one meeting and now carry the remnants of that into the next meeting? What will that do to your impact? And what if your most important senior stakeholder is in that next meeting? How*

will they see you? Is that the impression you want to make
and will your impact be the most positive and powerful it
could be? Will it create the outcome you want?

If you are running from meeting to meeting, it takes you only
a minute to stop and take a deep breath and think *how do*
I want to be in this meeting, not just *what do I want to do.*
How you are and how you come across is the biggest part of
your impact.

What do more senior people need?

Well, of course, ultimately, they want to see results, tangible
business results linked to the vision and strategy. They want
to see the links and connections to those results with context
too. So ensure that you are making the links. It may seem
obvious to you but may not be obvious to them.

They need to see that you are confident, that you can do
the job and that you can deliver solutions for them. Senior
leaders want to know that you are someone they can
delegate to and someone they can trust.

Keeping yourself at a strategic level will keep them engaged
and they are more likely to want to hear more from you.

Do not be afraid to share different thoughts, come up
with new ideas and be forthcoming with those. Leaders
want people to be giving fresh and new perspectives,
demonstrating a sense of creativity. Leaders cannot and do
not need to have *all* the answers.

A story of impact: Helmut opens up

Helmut was a very senior leader. He was seen as being
bottom-line driven: he was tough and demanding of his
people, always showing a very rational and logical side to

➤

everyone. The advice in the organisation from people who worked with him was to stay on the topic, not get side tracked, not to get involved in small talk and stay focused on what he wanted and needed. Results, driving the people and the business hard, was on top of his agenda.

This behaviour meant that people working with Helmut were cautious to engage in any personal conversations. They would hold back from talking about the people aspects of the business and would not engage in any personal sharing; talking about the weekend was almost forbidden. They would not share anything openly or necessarily open up about the reality of the business.

Direct reports to Helmut would wait for him to create any form of small talk. When approaching him, they almost waited for permission and would hesitate to see if he would say 'How are you?' There was a fear because they did not think that Helmut was interested in any form of opening up.

At a team meeting, where the team started to share a bit more about themselves and did some exercises in getting to know each other, Helmut learnt a lot more about the power of his impact and the power of these personal interventions.

One of Helmut's team members engaged him in one of his favourite topics, skiing! He became highly animated, talking about his love for skiing, recommending a fantastic Italian skiing resort and many good restaurants, even getting excited about what to order for lunch while out on the slopes. This amazed the team. He became so passionate they almost could not stop him.

After the time the team spent together focusing on getting to know each other and strategically talking about 'how' they worked together, the bottom-line results over the coming months improved. Helmut wanted that to continue. Intellectually and logically, Helmut saw the reason to open up more to people and share a little more to allow people also to open up with him. He actually enjoyed those interactions when he allowed himself to and he also saw the impact on the team. He now had the ability to bring that behaviour out in them too.

Learning from this story

The leader has an impact on the team, which, ultimately, impacts the bottom line in terms of the behaviours. The impact of shifting a behaviour had an effect on the people and the business. There was more openness, which created more sharing and allowed for people to talk about what was really happening in the business. By knowing the leader at a more personal level, people felt more able to be open.

There are a number of lessons to learn from this story:

▍ **From the direct report's perspective,** you have an impact and effect by colluding with the behaviour of just being task-focused. People did not feel able to open up and talk freely but, when someone did, they were surprised at how open Helmut became; it was a pleasant surprise. There was a more positive impact here – by being courageous, they could have influenced Helmut and made this happen sooner.

▍ **From the senior leader's perspective,** you always have an impact, either positive or negative, or even neutral. In this example, Helmut was not aware of the effect he was having. It was not his intention to create this environment or to create a culture of not sharing what was really happening but, by being too focused on tasks, he made people feel like they could not talk about anything else. He was having a partially negative impact on them, the team around him, the people that he lead in the organisation as well as his reputation and brand. It was easy to fix, though, and it took a change in behaviour to make the difference.

Solutions and tools

Here are some practical solutions and tools for having a positive impact on people more senior than you.

1. Stakeholder planning

It is important not just to manage your stakeholders but to lead them, so plan your stakeholder approach. You need to practise both stakeholder leadership and management.

Your success at work largely will come down to how well you connect with the relevant people in an effective way. You need to build a network that helps you do your job now and in the future. So really take time to reflect on who your stakeholders are, some may not be obvious, so try and think wider and bigger than your current role. Think about the future and what you want to happen with your career and then think about who could influence that for you.

Put into practice this simple process of mapping out your stakeholders. Have a plan for how to approach them. You will need to understand them, understand what they need and want from you and identify what you need from them.

Take a look at the Stakeholder Map below and mark out your stakeholders. Where do they fit? Put names in the boxes.

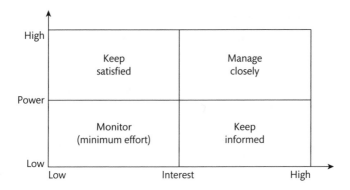

Stakeholder Map
Source: Mindtools.com

Then identify three to five key stakeholders where you need to build better relationships and then complete the plan.

Identify three to five critical stakeholders with whom you need to build better relationships	Name, role and why is this support so critical?	Support level: red, amber or green	Follow-up commitments/ actions
[KEY]Red = not supportive; amber = neutral; green = supportive			

Stakeholder leadership and management is important for all stakeholders and the steps here can be used for all, but, in this context, we recommend you focus on those more senior than you.

2. Stakeholder influencing

To be able to influence your stakeholders is another powerful step of stakeholder leadership. Like with everything else, some people will find it easy to influence and persuade others and some will need to put more work into it.

To influence at this level, you need to be able to make connections to the strategy and the vision and be able to convey that in a senior way.

Chunk up and down

Communicate with senior leaders by 'chunking' information up and down. Keep it concise and ensure you chunk the information up and down as needed. As a general rule, give the big picture with enough detail, but not too much. Be prepared to be flexible and adapt your style in the moment. Some leaders like the high level executive overview (chunking up) and some like the detail and specifics (chunking down). Figure that out and then adapt your style to what they need to give you more impact.

You will create a greater connection with a senior leader if you think about *how they* want the information not how you prefer to give it to them. Ask yourself: *How can I make them really want to hear what I've got to say?*

Use storytelling

All the way through this book, we are sharing examples of how impact works. This communication technique is simply called story telling. Most people relate more to stories and examples than to mere facts, so it is a great way of effectively engaging people. In stakeholder influencing, using stories is very helpful in getting your message across. So bring your information to life by using a story to illustrate a point. Senior leaders use stories too. Take the information you want to give, then think of an example you can use to make it come alive. You can also research stories to add value to your data.

Research shows that our brains love stories – and stories release oxytocin, a neurochemical responsible for empathy. According to Paul Zak,[12] oxytocin makes people more sensitive to social cues, which engages people in helping and supporting others.

Speak up

Sometimes people are fearful of speaking up to people more senior than them. They may be hesitant to share bad news or voice an opinion that is different from that of the senior person. This can be very counterproductive to innovation and great results. Do not just be a yes-sayer – remember that senior leaders depend on information to be able to make the big decisions. They depend on people closer to the business, closer to the customer to keep them in the loop of what is going on. When done in a collaborative, constructive, supportive and well-intended way, you also increase the chances of being heard and making them take on board your information or idea, hence having an impact as someone who dared to a make difference. When done in an effective way, it is a refreshing experience for those senior leaders.

The town hall: smart questions, not smart answers

JR was the new leader. To make an impact and a good first impression, he organised a town hall meeting with all of his new employees to let people know who he was and what he wanted to create for this business.

His team were gathered in front of him in the large auditorium, and he was really looking forward to this. He scanned the room; eager expressions on people's faces showed that his new team were keen to see what messages he was going to portray. JR took a deep breath and cleared his throat, he was ready to begin.

'Welcome to my first town hall meeting. I am delighted to be here with you today. I am excited about this business and

➤

want to share with you some of my thoughts on how I see this organisation in the future. Let me share with you what is really important to me.'

JR proceeded to talk about how passionate he was about the growth in the business, the opportunities in the global markets that he could see for them and the excitement about the clients and customers. JR was a great communicator and was enjoying the reaction he was getting from the people in the room. Some were nodding, some were smiling and others were watching him intently, waiting for what he was going to say next.

JR had the ability to make you feel like you were the only person in the room and that he was talking only to you. He was charismatic and was clearly very prepared for this meeting. He was really enjoying what he was saying, and you could tell he believed in it. JR was creating excitement and passion in the room. What he was saying was different, very different.

JR slowed down his words and took a look around the room, ready for the final section of his speech.

'I would like you all to close your eyes.' People quickly looked at each other. This is strange, they thought, what is he asking?

JR continued, 'I want you to imagine that it is three years from now. You are walking into the office, you are feeling good about coming to work. You are empowered to make decisions and you know what you are accountable for. You believe in the future and you want to work hard to achieve it. Now, tell me: what does that look like, what can you see, what does it sound like, what can you hear from others and what does it feel like for you? I want to hear your thoughts.'

There was a silence as people looked to each other for permission to speak. One person started and then people started to comment and call out their thoughts.

JR was delighted; he was happy with the way this meeting was going.

In this example, JR is showing great senior leadership qualities; he is a good communicator and a very good listener so he wants to hear from others about what they think and feel. He wants to engage them in what they want when it comes to working in a great environment, the one that he wants to create. He is involving people in thinking ahead. JR does not have all the answers.

The more senior you become, the more you do not need to have all the answers, nor would you be able to, even if you wanted. As a senior person, it is better to have smart questions than smart answers. In this example, JR could have just told them what it would look, feel and sound like in this great environment and culture that he wanted to create but that would not have engaged them in the same way as asking them some questions.

So, the more senior you become, the more you ask smart questions to allow others to learn and grow. If you do this, you will develop others. You also appear more senior. Of course, you have to have answers, but smart questions are sometimes smarter.

Practise your smart questions by adding these to your list:

▌ Tell me more about . . .

▌ In what way . . . ?

▌ How can that work . . . ?

▌ What else can happen . . . ?

3. **Use organic and reverse mentoring to help**

Mentoring is a superb way to connect with people more senior than you and reverse mentoring is a great process to use. This means that you are both learning from each other; you both take on the role of mentor and mentee.

Organic mentoring and reverse mentoring
Organic mentoring is when mentoring happens naturally, that is a person seeks out the guidance and support of

someone they would like to have as a mentor. It is organic; it meets the mentee's specific needs and it is driven by the desire of the mentee and the mentor – they both see the value and benefits of the mentoring relationship. And, when there is that shared desire to make it happen, it goes without saying that the results will follow. Reverse mentoring is simply ensuring that both people are learning from each other so the more senior person is learning as well as the person who is not as senior.

How to make your organic and reverse mentoring process a success

When considering a mentoring process, we recommend taking an approach that comes as close to organic mentoring as possible while, at the same time, providing the structure and support that is needed to make it as easy and effortless for the mentor and mentee to just get on with the mentoring.

An important part of kicking it all off is to have a very clear message and a communication strategy that ensures everyone involved really 'gets' the value of it. The communication should then continue throughout the mentoring timeline to help keep the momentum going, encouraging the participants to keep being proactive, looking for the continuous learning opportunities in the conversations with their mentor or mentee.

Another important ingredient is to prepare both mentors and mentees for their roles. This should include the following six-step process:

1.	Deciding on desired outcomes of the mentoring	What do you want to achieve by having a senior mentor?
2.	As a mentee	Deciding what experience/skills/ characteristics you know you can learn from and that you are, therefore, looking for in a mentor

3.	As a mentor	Thinking about what experience/ skills you have that may be of particular interest/value to the mentees in the mentoring programme
4.	Clarification of roles	What does it mean to be a mentor and what does it mean to be a mentee? What is expected of me?
5.	Considering how to structure the mentoring interaction for maximum benefit	For example: How long will it go on? How often will we meet/talk? What mentoring principles will we agree on? (e.g. confidentiality, etc.)
6.	Behavioural recommendations	For example: keeping an open mind, listening well, using critical thinking – and letting go of any need to 'be right', hence being truly open to the learning opportunity

In addition to this, we have noticed that the benefits for the mentor often are not highlighted enough, hence not getting to the full potential of the mentoring relationship. The mentor should get as much out of the mentoring as the mentee, as you learn a lot when you start sharing your experience and insights and can see it contribute to the mentor and his/her situation. We have found that mentors who start mentoring and realise that they will also go through a learning experience go from strength to strength. Reverse mentoring ensures this happens.

When this is done effectively, they are powerful and creative processes that can fast-forward the learning of all parties involved.

Be your own brand manager – 'behave as if you are'

Think of yourself as a brand and become your own brand manager. Whether you focus on it or not, you have a brand and a reputation This is really about taking control of your future and the way you are perceived. Your career is not just about a ladder going upwards but more about developing your skills, competencies and behaviours. This can happen by working more with your peers as well as your leaders. It is about how you develop and grow to be relevant in a changing environment. You never know when a peer will become your boss, so it is important to always think of your brand impact!

To raise your profile and brand (self-PR), it is much more effective to work on your behaviours than your task execution. How you act and behave matters greatly. Task execution is the expected minimum; behaviours will be the differentiating factor.

To progress and work on your self-promotion, we recommend practising the art of 'behaving as if you already are'. This works when done in an authentic way, when you are being true to yourself. If you are not a 'rah rah' person, then it will not work if you start shouting about what you are doing in a way that you would not normally do. It must be done in line with your authentic style.

To 'behave as if you are', you need to step into the shoes of the more senior person and ask yourself: *what would I do and how would I need to behave to be in that position?* If you observe people and you can see them 'behaving as if they are already in the job' (in an authentic way), it is obvious to others that they are ready and should be considered for the next job.

Here is a list of some behaviours you can use when 'behaving as if you are already'. Tick a few that are authentic to you, that you can try out.

- Be curious

- Be open-minded

- Be observant

- Be inclusive
- Be determined
- Be honest
- Be positive
- Be brave
- Be empathetic
- Be adaptable

The cross-calibration meeting

Stephen was leading the conversation at the cross-calibration meeting. At this meeting, all the senior leaders sat around a big table with a larger than normal spreadsheet in front of them. They also had a blank flipchart ready to collate their findings. The purpose of this session was to discuss all of their direct reports and discuss the performance along with their peers' performance to ensure there was consistency. There were always tough conversations at these meetings so there was some tension in the air.

Stephen started by talking about Anna. He was keen to get going.

'Anna has had a good year this year and I am delighted to say that she has exceeded all of my expectations. I have found her helpful and efficient, she has gone out of her way to be flexible and help other teams as well as delivering on her own work.'

Stephen was amazed at the reaction he got from his peers. Before he had even finished speaking, they were chipping in with comments on how they had found Anna very willing, how she had been solving challenges and problems in their teams too. Anna had been learning new skills by getting involved in tasks outside of her own area. She had been developing relationships with his peers by getting involved

➤

and sharing information with them and their teams too. It had all been noticed; she had done it in such a positive and natural way.

Stephen was putting Anna up for promotion. The promotion went through with no questions, it was well supported and there was a lot of positive feedback for her. Stephen could not wait to tell Anna about this great feedback. He wished the next conversation about Samuel was going to be as easy.

This meeting shows how senior leaders have conversations about their teams and share how they are performing. Anna has demonstrated how she is sharing ideas and showing that she is being creative and innovative in demonstrating that by helping others outside of her own area, while still performing. Anna has been good at self-promotion by building and developing good relationships, showing that she wants to constantly grow and develop. Anna has been positive, helped others, learnt new things and not been afraid of not knowing the answer. She has shown a belief in creating a learning culture.

Check in on your self-promotion. How are you doing?

4. Prepare for meetings – what to do, how to be

The more senior you are in an organisation, the more you need to prepare for meetings; that is obvious. What is not so obvious is how much time people prepare for how they are going 'to be' in a meeting, not what they are going 'to do'. Most people will spend around 100 per cent of their preparation time on what they need 'to do' in the meeting. They will be thinking about what they want to say and what the slides or communication needs to say and what the messages are.

Becoming more senior and behaving in a more senior way requires us to spend at least 50 per cent of the preparation time on how 'to be' in that meeting. Spending more time on these important aspects is key.

Imagine you are preparing to present at a quarterly business review and you are going to give an update on how the business is progressing/or your project or work is performing.

Work through the matrix below to plan for *'how do I need to be in this meeting?'*

Where shall I sit? Where do I position myself in the room?	Have I socialised some of these results to people in the room already to prepare them?	What else is on the agenda that I should know about?
Where shall I present from?	What frame of mind do I need to be in?	How do I position my story so that it is taken in?
Who will be in the room?	What do I want them to experience?	How shall I talk about the big picture and balance the detail?
Have I made the links to the strategy?	How shall I choose to influence the people in the room?	How can I include my peers? How can I ensure everyone is engaged?

This is not a finite list and you can create more 'how to be' reminders for yourself, depending on the meeting. The message is to spend more of your preparation time on how you need to be. Simply increase the time you spend on it to be more than it is now, to increase your positive impact.

Voice of impact

Impact is the feeling and response we create in others.

Here are some examples linked to this chapter of how an action or behaviour impacts people's feelings and therefore how they respond at work. This is how impact sounds and feels. They clearly show that what we do has consequences, good or bad. This gives us a greater understanding that we have the ability to affect our outcomes every moment of every day. This is a big responsibility and, as a leader, it is magnified through the wide sphere of influence that comes with a leadership role.

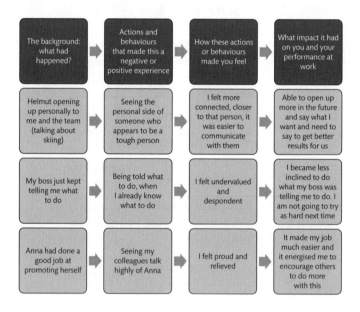

More solutions: the role your own thoughts, feelings and behaviours plays

When wanting to take control over your impact on people more senior than you, you first need to impact yourself.

> **What we think affects how we feel, and how we feel affects how we think.**

You can actively replace thoughts and feelings that are counterproductive to positive impact.

It is estimated[13] that a person experiences up to as many as 70,000 thoughts per day.

Many of those thoughts are habits that affect a person's mindset or outlook and, therefore, the impact they have on the world around them. It starts from within.

On the next page are some examples of negative thoughts, their impact on feelings and how they can be changed to new constructive thoughts to drive more effective impact behaviour.

Negative thought	Negative feeling	Ineffective behaviour	Constructive thought	Constructive feeling	Effective behaviour
Helmut is not interested in me	Distrust, fear	Withholding information, holding back	Helmut is interested, let me find a way to engage him	Supportive, trying to help	Creating more sharing and allowing for a learning approach
What value can I bring to this senior person? They know more than I do	Self-doubt	Lacking confidence, not stepping forward	How can I demonstrate what value I can bring to this conversation? I should focus on that	Positivity, more confidence	Volunteering information and daring to share a bold idea
I have to be right	Fear of not knowing	Not asking for input	I do not have to have all the answers. I trust myself	Curious	Asking questions and listening intently
I was worried about how my peers would react to my comments about Anna	Anxiety	Not being completely honest	I can be confident in my observations of Anna	Postive, calm	Sharing my observations and allowing for others to confirm my thoughts

Summary

If you are wanting to have greater, more targeted impact on people more senior than you, then start to pay more attention to it and be more intentional about creating that impact. Work through the solutions given, remembering to pay attention to your own state of mind and the role it plays. It does not have to be complicated; it is usually paying attention to the small things that gets great results.

This chapter also creates opportunities for you to reflect on and understand the impact you may be having on people more junior than you if you are a senior leader. Often your title goes before you so you have an impact just by walking into a room or attending a call. As a senior leader, you have a responsibility that goes with your position. So be aware of the impact you want to have and make sure it matches the reality.

THE EFFECT ON CULTURE

Culture is created every day, leader by leader. You help create the culture. If you want to have impact on a leader more senior than you, it is simple: behave in a way that influences the culture in a positive way. Be the change you want to see happen. The more you are able to impact also those more senior than you, the more you can influence the culture of the organisation, the way the organisation works. And a workplace where impact flows both up and down tends to be more inclusive and collaborative, which everyone can benefit from.

Self-assessment

After you have implemented the solutions in this chapter, answer these questions again to see the progress you have made.

How would you rate your ability to create impact on people who are more senior than you in these areas?

	1 Very poor	2 Poor	3 Just OK	4 Good	5 Excellent
Putting yourself in the shoes of stakeholders at a more senior level					
Asking smart questions as well as giving answers					
Being a mentor to others and learning from it yourself					
Behaving as if you are more senior					
Preparing for meetings on how you want 'to be' not what you want 'to do'					

If you think you're too small to have an impact, try going to bed with a mosquito.

Anita Roddick

5

Impact on people at the same level (peers)

LEADERSHIP FACT

Did you know?

A Gallup study of 7,272 US adults revealed that one in two had left their job to get away from their manager to improve their overall life at some point in their career.[14]

Self-assessment

Before reading this chapter, do the following quick self-assessment.

How would you rate your ability to create impact on peers in these areas?

	1 Very poor	2 Poor	3 Just OK	4 Good	5 Excellent
Treating peers like customers					
Giving credit to peers where credit is due					
Giving peer-to-peer feedback					
Being politically aware					
Seeking out learning opportunities with peers					

Exploring the stakeholder group: understanding your impact on your peers

It is at a peer level that a lot of organisational collaboration happens or should happen. It is also at a peer level that most competition or perceived competition happens. This means you immediately have a complex dynamic that needs to be considered carefully. There is nothing wrong with healthy competition that drives the business to a good place, but, when it moves into an 'outdoing each other' dynamic, it becomes unhelpful and disruptive to the business. Any short-term individual gain is a lose–lose in the long term. Collaboration is at the heart of successful physical and virtual workplaces.

Having watched the UK version of the reality TV series *The Apprentice* over the years has frequently made us reflect on what leaders and organisations can learn from their trials and tribulations.

In *The Apprentice,* the participants are a peer group divided into two competing teams. Each team really needs to work together to achieve tasks, with someone being chosen as the leader for each project. The two teams' results are then evaluated at the end of each project and one team wins, and at least one person on the losing team gets fired.

Here are our recent reflections on the peer dynamic.

The Apprentice

Watching *The Apprentice* is, sadly, often entertaining for all the wrong reasons. A lot of it is like a 'how not to behave in business if you want to impact others in a powerful and constructive way' master class that is being played out in all its glory.

We do understand that it needs to be entertaining and that participants are chosen with this in mind.

Here are five things *The Apprentice* candidates generally got wrong and five things they got right in one of the most recent seasons, from a teamwork, peer-to-peer and winning collaboration perspective. Most of these observations are trends that have been consistent over several seasons.

Five things they got wrong

1. Egocentric behaviours

Who wants to work with someone who is all about me, me, me? Egocentric behaviours where people keep promoting themselves, saying things like, 'I'm a natural born leader', 'no one is here to make friends' and 'I know I can beat anyone in this competition' are examples of this. Would you give it your all for someone who spoke like that? This egocentric outlook easily creates resentment in others and does nothing for team spirit.

➤

If you have to say, 'I am a natural born leader,' then you are likely not.

2. The blame game

As soon as things start to go badly, the candidates are quick to point the finger at each other, at their peers. Sometimes, this happens when the actual task is going on, but even more common is that it happens in the boardroom when people want to deflect negative attention away from themselves. The problem with the blame game is that it lacks personal responsibility and therefore leaves the person pointing the finger looking powerless. Respect is always possible in the boardroom, it is simply a choice of behaviour, and the best team members and leaders will always be respectful to others. As a peer, you never know when your peers will end up in a new and different position and even end up as your boss in the future.

3. Lack of planning

Many of the tasks are poorly planned. The teams quickly throw themselves into action mode, before first figuring out how they should operate together, how to communicate, report back, etc. There is not enough alignment between team members and sub-teams, making sure they know they are all working in the same direction. One example of this was when the teams were arranging the evening events and team members were off selling tickets at different prices and with different contents. Taking the time to plan, organise and align efforts are important parts of teamwork and collaboration. The best and most successful teams invest time in this critical part of the process.

4. Not recognising each other's strengths

People are not fully listening to each other or figuring out how to best to use the resources of the team. They all think they are there to promote themselves – and that is obviously, to some degree, how it has been sold to them, but no one is an island, no one can win a task on their own, just like in real life! For example, when the teams were creating a virtual reality game, the person who had the most experience in branding and graphic design was not put in charge of that task, and the outcome potentially could have been much more successful if those strengths had been valued and utilised. Using strengths in teams is a winning formula; using the people with the right skills for the job and acknowledging those strengths mean the task is performed more quickly, more productively and a better result is achieved. Within your peer group you can always use each other's areas of expertise or strengths to get you to collectively achieve more.

5. Poor communication

In pretty much every task, the sub-teams do not communicate enough with each other in order to align their purpose and their approach. As an example, when presenting their virtual game Magic Shells, no one knew who did what. It was chaotic and looked unprofessional. Feedback as a tool for great performance is also largely overlooked. They either do not give feedback at all (they just roll their eyes) or they scream in frustration; there is very little in between. And, as a result, no real change can happen, just conflict and friction. Finally, levels of listening are low, with candidates speaking over each other, resulting in them not hearing each other. Communication – or, more importantly, *two-way* communication – is crucial. In a peer group relationship, two-way communication can be used to ensure you are efficient and more aligned together. Really listening to others is the component to watch out for here.

Five things they got right

1. Having a clear goal

All tasks have a very clearly defined goal and success indicator. This helps them to start thinking about how to achieve that goal in the best possible way. With your peer group you can define goals, even if they have not been given to you or if they are just needed to pull you together. If there is no goal, then collectively agree on one.

➤

2. Appointing a leader

For teamwork to happen, especially when under time pressure, you need a leader to quickly get the team going. And this principle is used by *The Apprentice* teams as they discuss who is most suited for the role with regard to that particular task. The leadership role is alternated from task to task, providing the opportunity for benefits of shared leadership. This can be a good way of utilising strengths within your peer group. People often use this method, for example, when rotating the running or 'chairing' of a meeting. It is a good way to work with peers, as it builds trust and commitment.

3. Handling the fast pace

They are given very little time to carry out the tasks, just like how it can be in real life, and they show how it is possible to achieve results in a short period of time if you hustle. Using your peers to get things done at a quicker pace speeds things up.

4. Reviewing the results

It is good to review the outcome of a task or project, to figure out what went well and what did not. With peers, it is a good source of learning, and all results are a source of learning. By doing this, you are creating a culture of learning amongst your peers.

5. Celebrating success

The task winners always get a real boost from getting a treat and thoroughly celebrating their results. Sharing in a sense of pride that comes from accomplishment can really build a team.

The Apprentice is a great example of human interaction and how people impact one another in a high-paced, competitive environment. The candidates are all peers, where one of them now and then needs to step forward and take a leadership role. Hence there is a lot to be learnt from watching these interactions and reflecting on the impact they create, negatively or positively.

Let us look more closely at how peer competition and collaboration can play out and why it is so important to manage it.

Why are peers so important?

Leadership peers can often have shared leadership responsibility. This is particularly true for more senior leadership teams. In fact, in the future, successful companies will increasingly depend on leaders' ability to collaborate and practise shared leadership. There are several reasons for that, such as:

▌ The cultural trend is pointing in the direction of a more democratic, de-layered way of working. The McKenzie[15] model, 'the five trademarks of agile organisations', demonstrates how organisations are moving from the model of 'machines' to living organisms.

This describes organisations working like a machine with	Instead there is a shift to organisations working as living organisms with
Top down hierarchy type behaviours	Boxes and lines being less important, more working across boundaries of hierarchy
Bureaucracy ruling the workplace	Less important focus on action
Silo working being demonstrated	Quick changes with flexible resources
Employees been given detailed instruction	The leadership shows the direction and then allows for the actions
	Teams are built around end to end accountability to enable faster results

The agile organisation is dawning as the new dominant organisational paradigm
https://www.mckinsey.com/business-functions/organization/our-insights/the-five-trademarks-of-agile-organizations

▌ The speed of change means no one can have all the answers (including leaders). Increased collaboration is, therefore, a must.

▌ Increased collaboration and creative exchange make greater innovation a possibility.

A feedback culture

A former colleague of ours wanted to create a feedback culture by making feedback and performance reviews completely transparent. As a peer, you would be able to review, give feedback to anyone online and also be able to see what others had said about them. He was trying to create an environment where how people were performing was open and transparent. He wanted to make people more aware of how they were being perceived and what kind of impact they were having. His thinking was that greater transparency would make people think more carefully about their impact, not just moving into action without consideration of others. Clearly, this was a bold suggestion that many people would not be ready for, but we think it is great food for thought for all of us. What if there was that kind of transparency? In order to have respectful, powerful and constructive impact on my peers and beyond, what would I do differently and why?

Peers can be an invaluable community for airing your thoughts on challenges and frustrations, when you cannot share them with your boss or your direct team. So trust between peers is of massive importance. There are also a lot of opportunities for learning from each other, when the guard is down and trust is high. You need your peers, it is as simple as that.

We spend a lot of time at work, so why would you not make that an opportunity to engage rather than disengage with your peers?

You also do not know who is going to lead the team next or where that peer is going to end up next. They may even turn up as a client in the future, who knows! Think of your impact now and reap the benefits in both short and potential long term.

Be politically aware. Your peers can have a big impact on your career and your future. It is not uncommon that more senior leaders ask a leader's peers to give input on your effectiveness as a leader, on the results you are driving. This kind of input is often invited when career discussions are happening in cross-calibration and succession planning sessions. In fact, at any time when you or your career is being discussed, peers can be asked about your impact.

What do peers need?

They. Need. You.

There it is. No one can succeed alone. Whether they are fully aware of it or express it, they need collaboration, they need your input – all the things listed above. They need you to support them and they need you to ask for help. They need an exchange with you – general and regular or targeted and time-critical. Your knowledge, your experience, your ideas, your thoughts and your suggestions is what they need. When this kind of teamwork happens between same level leaders, you all achieve more: 1+1 = *at least* 3. The level and depth of collaboration decide the multiplying effect on your results. Give more, achieve more.

A story of impact: going it alone

Sophia was great at putting together presentations. She enjoyed it and she somehow assumed that others wanted her to take on that role too.

There was a big client meeting coming up where most of the responsibility resided in her area. Sophia wanted to be

➤

in control so she spent hours and late nights preparing, with data input from her own team.

Some of her peers would be in the client meeting and definitely had a role to play, but Sophia was keen to figure it all out on her own, thinking that her colleagues would appreciate that she took care of it and took ownership of the whole client proposition.

Sophia was used to seeing her peers as competitors and, as she had some doubt about her own capabilities, it was important to her to show everyone that she was as good as the next person. This meant doing plenty of research into all aspects of the subject, so that it would be obvious that she knew about even those aspects of the proposition that sat outside her area.

Christine had been thinking about the presentation and what to say and had some great ideas and was waiting for Sophia to contact her about it. And, being very busy, she had not got around to chasing Sophia.

The day had arrived. Sophia, Christine and their other three colleagues were all gathered in the meeting room together with the client group.

Sophia confidently presented the data and the clients loved it. They wanted to hear more and they wanted to carry on exploring it with her. Christine and the rest of her colleagues, on the other hand, were more frustrated about what was not there. The presentation had been good, but it could have been better with their input. They also felt excluded and snubbed.

In this story, Sophia does not tell her colleagues what she is doing. She should have involved her peers but, for various reasons, she did not. She did not fully trust the others, she thought she should be able to do it on her own and, as she thought the others were smarter, she felt she needed to have all the answers before involving them. She also did not involve them. In this case because she ran out of time – which could have been resolved if she had asked for help. Sophia's peers got frustrated because it felt like a 'tell' not an 'ask' when she finally approached them. She has, in theory, already thought about everything. But she has not; she needed their input and, hence, the results are not great. This has an impact on her peers: they do not feel included and they are not likely to rush to help her next time. She has started to erode trust, not gain trust, in this instance.

Solutions and tools

Here are some practical solutions and tools for having a positive impact on peers.

1. Treat your peers like customers

If you are not doing it already, start thinking about your peers like customers. Imagine that they are someone to whom you can be of service, someone you can help, someone you truly respect and for whom you want to do good things. And notice what happens. Impact starts in your mind; the way you think about someone drives your impact. If you do not like them or if you see them as a competitor, it will drive certain behaviours in you, subconsciously or consciously. Positive impact starts with how you think of your peers and is cemented through how you treat them.

A peer gets promoted

JR was a smart guy coming into the organisation. He was being talked about as someone who was going to be promoted, and everybody knew that about him. He came from a big firm with a great reputation and he had been very successful in his career in sales. JR came into his new team and focused on driving his own area and his own results, after all that was what his bonus was based on. He was seen as someone who was achieving but he was doing it on his own. He got good results and was well liked.

JR's peers were not that happy about his style because he did not seem to share with them how he was creating his success. He did not seem that happy engaging with them for meetings or taking time getting to know them and their customers. He definitely was not involved in helping his team members in anything that was not to do with his area or that would benefit his sales numbers.

Then the leader of the team got promoted and was given a bigger role in another region. Time for JR to shine. However, his peers were not keen about having him as their new boss so they were not supportive of him. When JR's peers were asked for their opinion on him, they gave feedback to say that, yes, he got good results but would he represent them well as a team and as individuals? He seemed to be interested only in his own results and that made them question whether he would be a good leader for them.

Another member of the team had been very collaborative with his colleagues and had been sharing some of his sales tactics, suggesting that they work together on joint customer initiatives and he seemed to have the interests of the team at heart. He said that he saw this team as his internal customers just as much as his external customers.

The question was, who was going to get the job of leading their peers?

2. Be generous with credit, stingy with blame

The blame game is an excellent way to have negative impact, so it is definitely something to avoid. Take personal responsibility by focusing on solutions rather than blame, if something goes wrong. And recognise the good things your peers do: praise constructive behaviour, give credit where credit is due. Never claim credit that is not yours. Be confident enough to lift others up and let them shine.

3. Give peer-to-peer observations

Figure out what each person is best at, what their strengths are. Then recognise those strengths when you observe them and give feedback on them. Everyone has a unique set of strengths, which are different from yours. The more you are aware of them, the more you can make the most of them, and highlight how you can achieve more as an organisation where everyone contributes the best of themselves. This reduces the risk of unhealthy competition as people feel unique and the need for such competition diminishes.

Feedback should, of course, also include development points. If you see that a colleague is having a negative impact on a situation through what they are doing, be honest and tell them. If you hesitate, consider that it is kinder to let them know than allowing them to continue repeating a behaviour that is not working for them. This *TOP feedback* model can help.

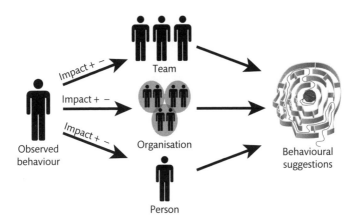

▌ Share your observation. What did you see them say, do, etc?

▌ Share the impact their actions and behaviours are having
on the team, the organisation and you. This model is
designed to make you think from all perspectives about
the impact on the team, the organisation and you. This
allows people to realise their impact on all of these
audiences and makes them think bigger.

▌ Suggest alternative (or similar – if positive feedback)
ways for future situations.

'What I really like about you, Samuel, is the amount
of knowledge that you have of this business and the
organisation. It has an impact on the team because we have
access to you, you can help us figure out a way around some
of the issues that we face. You know who to go to if we need
help. I would like to see more of it, though.'

JR took a sideways glance before he carried on.

'For the organisation, you are very experienced and that is
incredibly valuable. For me, personally, I am comfortable with
your level of understanding of our business and asking you to
help me out. Again, I want more of it and I would like to see
you volunteer that rather than me always having to ask you for
it. The impact on the team is that I don't feel you are a part of it,
you don't really support us. I would like you to feel more part of
this team. To the organisation, we don't appear to have a united
front and, as my peer, I am never sure how you represent us
to others.'

JR paused for a response.

4. Be politically aware

Develop your system thinking, to understand the 'system'
you are in. An organisation is an internal system, with
all its interrelated and interdependent parts: processes,

people, procedures, etc. The more you understand that system, the company culture, the rules and the undertones, the dynamics – the more impact you can have.

Have your radar on. You need to know the intricacies of who knows who, who is connected with whom. Who is collaborating with you? Who is competing with you? This is particularly important in the peer landscape where collaboration and healthy competition are a necessity for continuous creative challenge and growth.

The Political Skills Inventory,[16] based on research by Gerald R. Ferris and colleagues, identifies four distinct dimensions of political skills: social astuteness, interpersonal influence, networking ability and apparent sincerity. Further research shows that people skilled in these four areas positively impact job performance, influence, leadership and career advancement.

In the model below, reflect on each of these metaphorical 'political animals'. Where do you fit? You really want to be a wise owl who is very aware of where the clever foxes are.

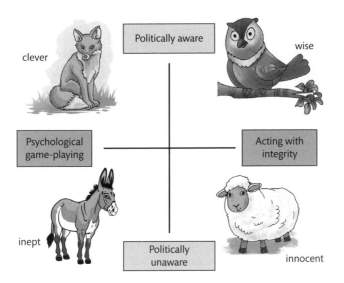

Wise behaviour is bringing together awareness with integrity. Here are six habits we recommend to succeed through political awareness.

Habit 1	Aim for win–win outcomes wherever possible
Habit 2	Be a keen observer, observe without judgement, aim to understand
Habit 3	Consider your impact, practise impulse control, think carefully about what you say and how you behave
Habit 4	Be authentic and sincere
Habit 5	Get your focus right, consider your circles of influence
Habit 6	Build collaborative and relevant relationships

5. Seek out learning opportunities with your peers

You know some things, your peers know other things. When you put that knowledge and experience together, you multiply it. Lead the way for this by generously sharing what you know.

▌ Make the most of the diversity that resides in your peer group.

▌ Ask for help.

▌ Invite and engage people into discussion, healthy debate and exchange.

▌ Take an active interest in others by asking them for their input and creative ideas.

▌ Assume positive intent too, that others mean well when they are sharing or hesitating to share (they may not be used to it).

By doing so, you open up to the other person. You look for the positive, the possibilities, and the possible connections into what you are doing. If someone is competitive, for example, see the positive intent behind that rather than going into a competitive mode yourself. Use questions to get a discussion going, rather than shutting the door to collaboration.

Workplace differences can be a good thing, a very good thing even, and definitely should not be feared but addressed. Managing peer conflict is everyone's responsibility. Peers and teams who have experienced conflict and resolved it grow stronger together. So do not fear conflict, welcome it for its innovative powers and use it carefully and respectfully.

Voice of impact

Impact is the feeling and response we create in others.

Here are some examples linked to this chapter of how an action or behaviour impacts people's feelings and therefore how they respond at work. This is how impact sounds and feels. They clearly show that what we do has consequences, good or bad. This gives us a greater understanding that we have the ability to affect our outcomes every moment of

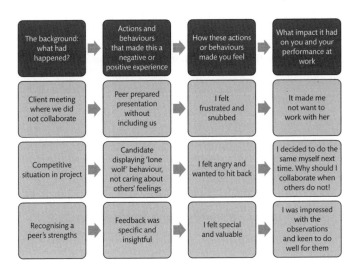

every day. This is a big responsibility and, as a leader, it is magnified through the wide sphere of influence that comes with a leadership role.

More solutions: the role your own thoughts, feelings and behaviours play

When wanting to take control over your impact on employees, you first need to impact yourself.

> **What we think affects how we feel, and how we feel affects how we think.**

You can actively replace thoughts and feelings that are counterproductive to positive impact.

It is estimated[17] that a person experiences up to as many as 70,000 thoughts per day.

Many of those thoughts are habits that affect a person's mindset or outlook and, therefore, the impact they have on the world around them. It starts from within.

On the next page are some examples of negative thoughts, their impact on feelings and how they can be changed to new constructive thoughts to drive more effective impact behaviour.

Negative thought	Negative feeling	Ineffective behaviour	Constructive thought	Constructive feeling	Effective behaviour
It was his fault!	Anger	Pointing a finger in blame	I'm sure he did the best he could	Empathy	Looking for solutions
She didn't tell me what she was doing – again!	Indignation	Taking revenge by not telling what I am doing	She must have overlooked telling me (assume positive intent)	Understanding	Explain why including me is so helpful – for us both
I can't share that with them – that will give them an advantage!	Fear, jealousy	Holding on to valuable knowledge and experience	If I share that, we will both learn and benefit	Hopeful	Generous sharing

Summary

Shared leadership is increasingly necessary for successful organisations. Different people need to step forward at different times, to lead the peer group to success. Different people will be best suited to take the lead at different times. Powerful, impactful peer groups understand this. The leadership role is alternated from task to task, providing the opportunity for benefits of shared leadership.

To increase your impact with your peers, look for the common purpose, what you have in common. *What do you all want to achieve?* And then talk about that and reach agreement on a shared commitment to that purpose. Whenever possible, connect your goals to those of your peers. If there are competitive behaviours between you and your peers, then having connected goals will make those competitive behaviours impossible to carry on with. If each peer team member can be goaled not just on his/ her individual performance but also the performance of the team overall, then it brings out collaborative behaviours instead.

THE EFFECT ON CULTURE

A peer group can have a collective impact on the culture in an organisation. A strong and aligned group of collaborative peers will impact the culture in a team, department or even the organisation as a whole. With your peers you can even define and explicitly talk about the type of culture that, collectively, you want to create. Working constructively together will multiply the positive impact on the culture. You will be creating a culture whether you realise it or not, so you may as well be intentional about it.

Self-assessment

After you have implemented the solutions in this chapter, answer these questions again to see the progress you have made.

How would you rate your ability to create impact on peers in these areas?

	1 Very poor	2 Poor	3 Just OK	4 Good	5 Excellent
Treating peers like customers					
Giving credit to peers where credit is due					
Giving peer-to-peer feedback					
Being politically aware					
Seeking out learning opportunities with peers					

Success is not measured in the amount of dollars you make but the amount of lives you impact.

Anonymous

6 Impact on the board of directors

Self-assessment

Before reading this chapter, do the following quick self-assessment.

How would you rate your ability to create impact on the board of directors in these areas?

	1 Very poor	2 Poor	3 Just OK	4 Good	5 Excellent
Demonstrating confidence					
Inspiring and relating					
Communicating and coaching					
Relating to vision and strategy					
Showing respect					

Exploring the stakeholder group: understanding your impact on the board of directors

A board is a group who meets regularly to review the performance and strategic progress of the company. The board provides strategic leadership for your organisation and holds leaders in the organisation accountable for the running of it.

Boards are usually made up of independent directors (non-executive directors) and owner and operator directors. Non-executive board members are, typically, seasoned leaders who have an executive role in another organisation or have had. Being a 'board pro', .i.e having a number of non-exec director roles as a career, is increasingly becoming a career direction for many senior leaders.

The board needs to be able to separate itself from the everyday aspects of the business and take a helicopter view of the business. Boards come in different shapes and sizes as it depends on the business and needs of that business. No matter what that board looks like, you have to have the ability to impact the board at certain times. And, when that opportunity arises, no matter how frequent or infrequent, you need to be ready.

Having experience at an executive level and having been able to secure an executive or non-executive board role probably means that this person also has plenty of executive presence. Or, as it is sometimes called, 'gravitas'. Executive presence is a combination of behaviours, skills and style, and sometimes can be described as the ability to command a room (sometimes without saying or doing anything), to make everyone aware that you are someone in charge. We will explore executive presence and its importance, for all leaders, in this chapter.

Why is the board so important?

The board are often more senior than leaders in the organisation, which means that you are leading upwards when you deal with them. However, there is a distinction between the board and the senior leaders we talked about in Chapter 4. Board members are there to steer from a strategic viewpoint, typically not getting involved in the day-to-day operation of the organisation.

You need the board onside if you are proposing a change to your organisation's focus and operations. Whatever leadership role you are in, you are closer to the reality of the day-to-day running of the business. You will need to be able to present and convey such changes in a cohesive and persuasive way. You need to communicate with the board on their level to be able to get them to hear and see the potential in new or even disruptive ideas. You need to show the potential strategic impact of what you suggest.

Getting heard by the board

We worked with a CEO who wanted to make a big strategic change and who had to work hard to make herself heard by the board. Her learning was that she had to prepare thoroughly to get her own head out of the details and look much more at the bigger picture of the strategic direction set and how what she was proposing might disrupt that direction. In this case, she was looking for a disruption and the kind of preparation she had to make, with scenario planning and market research, was extensive. It paid off, though – the board were convinced that the new strategy was worth pursuing.

What does the board need?

The board needs reassurance that the organisation is run in an efficient and business-viable way. Its members need to feel trust in the leaders of the organisation and that they are carrying out the strategic direction in line with the company vision and values.

The board needs continuous updates from the frontline of the organisation, to stay informed and to be able to make strategic considerations and decisions. Board members, the chairperson in particular, also need to manage their part of the relationship to stakeholders and press, hence the need for transparency into the reality of day-to-day business. In an increasingly digitalised and automated world of digital transformation and artifical intelligence, the board particularly needs to educate itself in these areas, with the help of experts within the organisation.

A high-performing company must ensure the relationship between the board and leadership is complimentary rather than adversarial. This is one of the most important relationships within a company, so make sure it is well managed. Think about your role in this when you are interacting with and impacting the board.

It is easy to get confused with the difference between governance and leadership. The board is in charge of governance of a company that seeks to ensure the smooth running of a business by making accountability and oversight the core of their workings. Governance also ensures that the business has a future-facing strategic plan. So, when you impact a board, you have to stay in this future-facing strategic mindset space yourself.

This is where leadership comes in. Executive and operative leaders take the strategic plan and implement it into the everyday operations of the company. Both governance and leadership roles are vital and totally complement each other.

A story of impact: a seat at the table

When we were working with an executive director who was struggling in the board room, we talked to her about what she was thinking during her interventions in that boardroom. To start with, she did not see herself as having a seat at the table, quite literally. There were never enough seats for everyone, so she ended up being at a seat at the side of the table, even away from the main board table.

She had to take more responsibility for her positioning in this important session. We worked with her to really work through where she wanted to position herself in the room, who she sat next to, who she sat opposite and who she needed to gain eye contact with to influence more. All of this meant she was more intentional with her role in the boardroom. She arrived early, sat in the right space at the table, thinking carefully about who she was next to and where she needed to be. She prepared more for 'how' she was going to say what she wanted to say as well as 'what' she wanted to say. This made her feel more 'at the table' and more able to present her thoughts and views in a powerful way. It helped her to integrate into the board and have more of a voice to be listened to, resulting in her getting feedback to say she was having a bigger impact on the board.

Executive presence as an impact tool

Effective executive presence can look different in different leaders. Some exude it, regardless of what position they have. So what is it? How would you describe it? And how do you get it and develop it, if it is not already there?

Exuding executive presence

We were recently in a situation with 50 leaders in a room where a senior leader was joining us, whom we had not previously met. As soon as she entered the room, we could tell it was her by the way she strode in, confidently, her eyes were scanning the room, smiling, nodding and acknowledging people's presence, indicating that she had seen them and would get to them.

She moved easily to her seat and started a conversation with the people at that table; interested, engaged. The way people reacted when she arrived confirmed who she was to us. They turned their attention towards her, almost straightening their posture in their chairs and clearly signalling that they knew she was there. Some were even getting up and walking up to her, extending a hand, hence demanding her attention. Others sat back, but their radar was still on with regard to where she was. She became the focus of attention, whether she wanted it or not.

Even if she had not had executive presence, she would have attracted their attention because of her position. There is always positional presence, dictated by the seniority of the role, but executive presence is about more than a title and hierarchy.

We are talking here about effective executive presence, needed to build relationships and long-term success. Many of us may have experienced not such positive executive presence, where leaders have used their position of power to dominate, instil fear and influence in a manipulative and negative way. In the story above, the senior leader could have had a very different response from people if she had stormed into the room, on her phone, still talking, acting superior and only wanting to talk to the more senior people, for example. It would have made people feel unimportant, not respected and not appreciated. Back in the workplace, this would lead to you not wanting to go the extra mile for that leader, so productivity would be negatively affected. There would, arguably, have been some kind of executive presence but not of the kind that drives trust and sustainable collaborative followership. *There is nothing endearing about dictatorial leadership.*

So, when you are in a position to influence a board or a senior leadership team, then you have to work on your own traits and behaviours. Spend just as much time on 'how' you need to be as well as 'what' you need to do.

Having executive presence and gravitas becomes the key factor to use in order to influence more and more effectively. Here are a number of traits and behaviours that often are experienced with executive presence and gravitas. Review them and reflect on how consistently you display these today and which ones you need to be more intentional about. To get the most out of this, be really honest with yourself. No one does these things perfectly, everyone will have aspects they can improve on. As you reflect on the traits and behaviours, put them into a specific, regular or particularly important context so that the assessment becomes as relevant as possible.

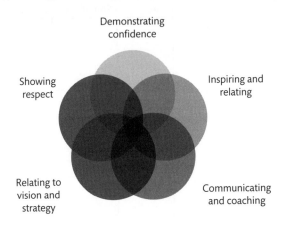

Demonstrating confidence

Showing respect

Inspiring and relating

Relating to vision and strategy

Communicating and coaching

The Executive Presence Sweet Spot™

Demonstrating confidence

Traits/behaviours	In the context of your executive presence and the impact you have, how consistently do you think you display these traits/behaviours?		
	Rarely	Sometimes	Always
Being self-assured and confident with who they are			
Being authentic, feeling comfortable with who they are			
Taking things on, without asking for permission			
Having belief in themselves and their abilities			

demonstrating confidence cont. . .

Traits/behaviours	In the context of your executive presence and the impact you have, how consistently do you think you display these traits/behaviours?		
	Rarely	Sometimes	Always
Knowing that their impact is their legacy, that what they do today can have a lasting impact			
Showing their passion			
Not feeling the need to over-explain things			
Knowing what their brand is, what they want to be known for			
Not being afraid to take pride in great results (taking the victory lap)			
Hiring people smarter, more knowledgeable than themselves			

Inspiring and relating

Traits/behaviours	In the context of your executive presence and the impact you have, how consistently do you think you display these traits/behaviours?		
	Rarely	Sometimes	Always
Being a realistic optimist			
Instilling hope in others			
Being firm but fair, and empathetic			
Investing in relationships with stakeholders			

Inspiring and relating cont. . .

Traits/behaviours	In the context of your executive presence and the impact you have, how consistently do you think you display these traits/behaviours?		
	Rarely	Sometimes	Always
Being a human being at work (not a 'human doing'), being authentic and focusing on the human to human (H2H) interaction			

Communicating and coaching

Traits/behaviours	In the context of your executive presence and the impact you have, how consistently do you think you display these traits/behaviours?		
	Rarely	Sometimes	Always
Listening without prejudice			
Knowing when to wrap up dialogue and move forward			
Asking smart questions, not always giving the answers			
Not having to have all the answers			
Teaching others 'how to fish'; not telling people how to do it, but letting them find their own way			
Having experience and sharing that wisdom			
Being a mentor to others, resulting in learning for both the mentee and mentor			

Relating to vision and strategy

Traits/behaviours	In the context of your executive presence and the impact you have, how consistently do you think you display these traits/behaviours?		
	Rarely	Sometimes	Always
Thinking bigger and seeing the bigger connections			
Having a vision and being able to articulate it, and getting people to connect with it			
Being transparent, not having a hidden agenda			
Having belief in a bigger purpose and a passion for the vision			
Ability to see how things are connected, making the links for others too			
Making well-informed, considered decisions			
Being intentional, strategic, mindful in how they approach their interactions and communication (not being a 'loose cannon')			

Showing respect

Traits/behaviours	In the context of your executive presence and the impact you have, how consistently do you think you display these traits/behaviours?		
	Rarely	Sometimes	Always
Giving other people credit where credit is due			

showing respect cont . . .

Traits/behaviours	In the context of your executive presence and the impact you have, how consistently do you think you display these traits/behaviours?		
	Rarely	Sometimes	Always
Paying attention to the important things, e.g. getting people's names right			
Being aware of the political landscape, not playing political games but being aware of how it all works			
Navigating the political landscape in a respectful way			
Taking and expecting responsibility without blaming (fostering a no-blame culture)			
Winning the respect of their peers			

How did you do?

Whatever the results, that is just your own self-assessment. It is a good start and, to get a more complete picture, you may need to validate it with others. What are they experiencing? Ask for feedback, particularly if there are areas where you are unsure about how consistently you embody those specific traits or behaviours. Build a solid understanding of these areas of impact so you can make the most of them.

Once you have done that, identity which of these five areas you want to work on to increase your executive presence. Then apply the relevant tools below.

Solutions and tools

Here are some practical solutions and tools for increasing your executive presence and, therefore, having a positive impact on the board and others you need to influence with your presence.

1. Demonstrating confidence

Confidence comes from within. You need to feel it to be able to demonstrate it. Here are three steps to building that confidence so it shows.

▌ Set time aside to review weekly or monthly what you have achieved, how far you have come. It is easy to forget unless you stop and take stock and take it onboard as a feeling, cementing the experience in your body. *What wins have you had? What relationships have you built? What milestones have you completed? Who will you celebrate with? Who do you need to thank?*

▌ Take control of your physical appearance: your attire, your personal grooming. Consider who your audience is and dress in keeping with the situation and setting. All of this adds up to your visual presence.

▌ Choose your power stance and where you choose to sit or stand in the room. Claim your space by being powerfully present. Consider your posture, your facial expressions and gestures. Are you looking people in the eyes or looking away? Is your back straight and head high? Is your voice clear and strong?

2. **Inspiring and relating**

Focusing on the problem

Samuel was asked to attend the monthly senior leadership meeting to give an update on the digitalisation project and the progress that the IT department had been making. Samuel started by telling everyone what was going wrong with the project, why it had gone wrong and whose fault it was.

He would be asked often to attend these meetings to represent his department and he would not say anything unless he saw an issue or had a challenge. JR was getting tired of this and decided to raise this with Samuel's boss, Stephen. Because Samuel spoke only when there was a problem or issue, the team were starting to think that Samuel *was* the problem. This caused his reputation to suffer and the senior leader stopped asking him for his input.

The more senior you become, the more you look for what is wrong, to resolve major issues. You are often a problem solver, which means you see the problem. This means often you are looking at the critical flaws of something. You need also to reinforce and increase the positives and get people focused on the opportunities for innovation and growth. You need to inspire people to see future possibilities and create solutions for it.

▎ To inspire hope, look for what can go right (not what can go wrong). De Bono's Thinking Hats[19] is a great tool to use here. It is a process aimed at forcing people to consider an idea from various different angles, to get to as much information as possible before making a decision. The Yellow Hat in particular stands for brightness and optimism and, when 'wearing' it, you think only of all the good things something might bring, all the opportunities it could create.

▌ Show people something of your authentic self. Decide what you want to share about yourself to others today, to make people connect with the person that is you. Choose things that convey something personal about you, such as a hobby, your family, where you live and why you live there, etc.

▌ Decide what you could ask others to get to know them better. Choose things to which you are genuinely interested in hearing the answer. How about: *What made you choose this particular career path? What do you enjoy the most about your job? What is your big interest or hobby?*

3. Communicating and coaching

Reaching other people through communication is something we do every day. The ability to convey a message in such a way that the other party takes it in the way it was intended is a skill that can be practised and perfected. This is also what coaching is all about: encouraging someone to reflect on feedback and results and grow and develop:

▌ Ask great questions. Great leaders ask really smart questions – they do not always give the answers. They realise that the art of asking questions is crucial in creating engaged team members. Think about it – when someone asks you a question and they are being genuinely interested and listening – how great does that feel! It makes you feel seen and important, it makes you want to get involved. It also makes you learn, as it gets you to explore and think of potential answers.

▌ A leader definitely does not need to have all the answers, she/he just needs to have really smart questions. In fact, it can be easy to give the answer. It is more challenging to think of a smart question that allows the other person to think about the answer and for the leader to think about how the answer will get the person thinking differently. Here are some of our top tips to consider

▌ What is the purpose of the questioning? This is important so that you can target your questions at that purpose.

▌ Open or closed questions? Open questions gather more information, but there are times when a quick yes or no is all you need or have time for – and then a closed question is the best option.

▌ Use softening phrases. Posing too many questions can sound like an interrogation, so think about how you can best frame the question to make it interesting for the other person to answer it. Here are some examples of softening phrases to start your question sentence with: *I'm curious . . . ; I'm really interested in your thoughts on . . . ; Tell me more about . . .*

Ask the question (with softening phrases, if relevant). Here are some examples of great open questions: *What do you think we should do next? What would you recommend?*

If you could do anything, what would you do?

Where could we find that information, do you think?

▌ The most important thing – *listen.* Do not think about how you will respond to what is being said – just listen. It is amazing to see what happens when we fully listen to other people.

▌ Thank them. Whomever you have talked to, whatever the subject – thank them. Make sure they know that you really appreciate their input. Do this in an authentic way.

▌ Think about how to make the most of the insight you have had from talking to others. Consider the different views you have been privy to. Do not forget to formally credit those that have given input, if relevant.

▌ So think about it – who will you be meeting with today, tomorrow or next week? What questions can you prepare to make that meeting interesting and rewarding for you both/all?

▌ When someone asks you a question, practise stopping yourself from simply giving the answer straight away and, instead, think about how you can create a dialogue that involves the other party in finding the answer.

▌ Bring the customer to the board. Bring stories of customer experience to the board members – share representative examples and data that paints as complete a picture as possible.

One of our clients started bringing in a customer story to each board meeting; the board enjoyed it so much and gained a lot from it, so our client now brings an employee story too.

▌ Think about how to break through and really claim the attention you want to have when communicating with the board and its members.

A challenging presentation

In a recent board meeting that we were observing, a senior leader from the organisation that reported to the board was asked to join the meeting to present to the board. The presenter walked into the room. First, the board were late and had made him wait outside for 20 minutes. When he came in, he handed out his presentation. The board pounced on the paper. All heads were down and they were reading ahead and already asking questions before he had even started talking. There was no eye contact from the board or apology to him for being so late. They jumped in. After constantly being interrupted and challenged, his time was up. The chairperson said a quick thank you and summed up the next steps. They literally dismissed him and moved on with their agenda.

I followed the presenter out of the room. I asked an extremely open question, 'How did you find that?' 'It was tough. They didn't even wait for me to present and it was like being in a "den of wolves" with question after question. I was going to get to all of their questions as it was part of my presentation, but they didn't let me. They started arguing amongst themselves and there wasn't any acknowledgment for the work I had done. I have worked on this for six months. I feel deflated and I am certainly not in a hurry to go back to the board again. In fact, what value did they add to me as the board? Not a lot.' With shoulders slouched, he hurried off down the corridor as fast as he could.

In this example, the board definitely had an impact on the presenter and they needed to be aware of that impact. The presenter also had an impact and could have taken more control and influence too. There were good learnings for all.

▌ Volunteer to be a mentor. If there is a mentoring scheme at work, offer your services to it. Become a generous sharer of your knowledge, skills and experience.

4. **Relating to vision and strategy**

Start operating at the level you want to be at or that of the person you want to have an impact on. Behave as if you are already at that level. Think bigger, leave your operational and tactical head at the door. Push yourself to be more visionary and strategic.

▌ Prepare for what you are going to say in a meeting, and how you need to be. What impact are you going to have? What do they need to see and experience that will give a better result?

▌ Rehearse and practice ahead of important meetings, such as board meetings. Engage a trusted peer and ask them to give feedback on your impact.

▌ Make a habit of practicing asking strategic questions. Here are some examples you can pick from to get your started:

  ▌ For what purpose are we doing that?

  ▌ What are going to be the long-term benefits?

  ▌ How will the organisation be impacted?

  ▌ How will that affect our culture?

  ▌ Are we being customer-focused enough? What do our customers want?

  ▌ What is the competitive landscape like? What do our competitors say?

  ▌ Who are the most important stakeholders and what do they need over time?

5. Showing respect

When shown respect, people respond with respect and a willingness to engage and cooperate. Respect could be like the Golden Rule: 'treat people as you would want to be treated', but it could also go a step further, like the Platinum Rule: 'treat people as they would want to be treated'. The difference lies in not assuming that people are all the same, but that, in reality, each person is unique and that it is respectful to notice and honour those differences.

▌ Do not waste people's time. Be someone who makes people feel like they have been given time. Do not be a stealer of time. Add value by getting the focus and level of detail right, staying focused on the subject and managing the time, making it easier for people to do a great job.

The time stealer

Sophia was travelling on business and was currently in Boston. It was 5 am in the morning and she was waiting for a call. The HR leader in Europe was calling to ask for feedback on a member of Sophia's team. Sophia had only 30 minutes available in her day and this was it. The phone bleeped at the exact time of 5 am. Sophia got straight into the dialogue about the person.

'The challenge is that he is a "time stealer",' Sophia said.

'What do you mean? Can you explain more?' said the eager HR leader.

Sophia continued, 'Well, for example, if I ask him a question, he takes a long time to answer it, as he explains it over and over again. He takes up too much of my time, he steals my time. Whereas, right now, I know you are going to be concise with me and to the point and that means you will give me back 10 minutes of my day by finishing this call early, so you are not stealing my time.'

In this example, Sophia, as a busy senior leader and board member, needs people to be concise and to the point, as she has no time to spare and, when she gets that, she is able to complete her goals for the day.

▌ Understand the political landscape at the board level – what do they want and need from you? Recognise what operational excellence looks like for them and deliver that – build their trust in you by giving them what they need and ask for.

▌ Never blame and point a finger at others when things do not go to plan. Look instead for solutions by having good question or dialogue prompters, such as:

▌ What can we do differently going forward?

▌ What can we learn from this?

▌ What if we could . . . ?

▌ Next steps could involve . . .

▌ What new ideas has this given us?

Voice of impact

Impact is the feeling and response we create in others.

Here are some examples linked to this chapter of how an action or behaviour impacts people's feelings and, therefore, how they respond at work. This is how impact sounds and feels. They clearly show that what we do has consequences, good or bad. This gives us a greater understanding that we have the ability to affect our outcomes every moment of every day. This is a big responsibility and, as a leader, it is magnified through the wide sphere of influence that comes with a leadership role.

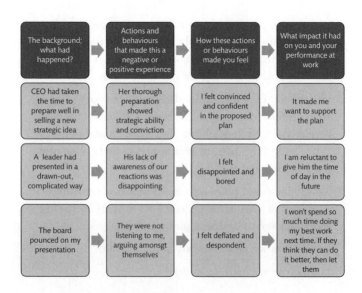

More solutions: the role your own thoughts, feelings and behaviours play

When wanting to take control over your impact on board members, you first need to impact yourself.

> **What we think affects how we feel, and how we feel affects how we think.**

You can actively replace thoughts and feelings that are counterproductive to positive impact.

It's estimated[20] that a person experiences up to as many as 70,000 thoughts per day.

Many of those thoughts are habits that affect a person's mindset or outlook and, therefore, the impact they have on the world around them. It starts from within.

On the next page are some examples of negative thoughts, their impact on feelings and how they can be changed to new constructive thoughts to drive more effective impact behaviour.

Negative thought	Negative feeling	Ineffective behaviour	Constructive thought	Constructive feeling	Effective behaviour
The board members are so far removed from reality	Suspicion	Not engaging enough with the board members	What can I do to bring the reality to the board? What do they need from me?	Empowerment, hope	Active engagement, asking board members what they need
It is not OK to challenge the status quo	Fear	Ideas are not expressed	How can I challenge the status quo in a way that others want to listen to?	Hope	Creatively challenge the status quo
I cannot be myself, I need to just fit in	Self-doubt	Holding back, not expressing different views	I have something unique to contribute and I am confident that it adds value	Positivity	Appreciating differences, trying something new

Adjusting the self-image

Anna was at the monthly board meeting again. Why am I here? she thought to herself. What am I doing here? I don't *do* anything when I am here, what value am I adding?

This was a common feeling for Anna to have. We worked with Anna to coach her to understand how to build confidence in these board sessions.

'so, what are you thinking and feeling when you are in these meetings?' I asked.

Anna started to unravel why she felt this way at the board meeting.

'Well, when I go into a board meeting, I just think I am the admin assistant in the room. I started as an admin assistant and, yes, I have worked my way to chief executive now and I am on the board, but I still see myself as that admin assistant.'

Anna had worked her way up through the organisation and was still seeing herself as she was many years ago and not as she is today.

'Well, what do you think the others in the room think when they see you? Do you think they see the admin assistant or the chief executive?' I probed.

'I guess they don't know the admin assistant, but I still see myself as Anna just doing what Anna does,' she replied.

'When you were the admin assistant and the chief executive walked in, what did you think and how did you behave?' I continued.

'I used to think, "that is the chief executive, so the fact that they are here, in the room and present is enough before they even speak". So, with that in mind, I guess I have more presence than I think and, with that, comes responsibility too. And that applies to the board as well for me, doesn't it?' She smiled, she was asking herself a rhetorical question as the realisation hit.

Summary

The board and its members are your organisation's strategic advisors. Your ability to interact effectively with them, as/when needed, is a necessity. You need them and they need you. Remind yourself what they need from you – concise, thoughtful intel from the business – and deliver it. Your professional delivery helps them make those strategic decisions and provide guidance for the road ahead.

Research from around the world shows that many boards are non-diverse (with regards to gender, ethnicity, background, age, etc.), many of them being referred to as 'male, stale and pale' (*The Sunday Times,* 2017)[21] and 'male, stale and frail' (*Financial Times,* 2016).[22] This may mean that boards could be in danger of practising 'group think', following the same pattern of thinking and reasoning. A fast-changing world demands continuous challenging of the status quo and even disruption to create relevance for the future and long-term, sustainable success.

Giving Helmut a helping hand

Stephen had a dilemma. His boss Helmut had recently accepted an appointment to the board of directors at another company. This had prompted a more and more prevalent thought – why are there so many older men on boards? He agreed with the sentiment and recognised that the board Helmut was joining was not particularly diverse. They all had similar backgrounds and he realised that they might be at risk of 'group thinking', where similar backgrounds and ages meant there may be similarities in values and thought processes.

The company was planning some major digital upgrading and the board needed to step up to the plate and help role model the type of learning culture they would need to be able to achieve that transformation. Stephen realised that he could play a role in this by trying to influence Helmut to see this dilemma and to challenge creative dialogue and new thinking from the start of his board service. As Stephen had got better and better at 'speaking Helmut's executive language', he decided to have a word with Helmut and encourage him to bring real value to the board he was joining.

THE EFFECT ON CULTURE

Ultimately, the board are also responsible for the culture they help create. They have to be custodians of the culture. As there can be that natural tension on the board, between the practicalities of guiding the business here and now *and* for the future, then to influence the board you have to help them see the culture they are creating through their decisions. You can help with the reality of how the culture is and how any big future changes will impact the culture. You can be the reality check for the board, which really adds value. So, reflect on how you can affect the board's thinking about culture. What impact can you, in turn, help *them* to have?

Self-assessment

After you have implemented the solutions in this chapter, answer these questions again to see the progress you have made.

How would you rate your ability to create impact on the board in these areas?

	1 Very poor	2 Poor	3 Just OK	4 Good	5 Excellent
Demonstrating confidence					
Inspiring and relating					
Communicating and coaching					
Relating to vision and strategy					
Relating to vision and strategy					

The art of communication is the language of leadership.

James Humes

7

External Impact with stakeholders, media/ press, social media

Self-assessment

Before reading this chapter, do the following quick self-assessment.

How would you rate your ability to create impact on external stakeholders and the world around overall in these areas?

	1 Very poor	2 Poor	3 Just OK	4 Good	5 Excellent
Choosing behaviours that make the difference					
Considering your impact on customers and their experience					
Working effectively with your partners, suppliers, subcontractors, etc.					
Managing the media/press					
Social media and brand management					

Exploring the stakeholder group: understanding your impact on external stakeholders and the world around you

Why are they so important?

Transparency and the expectations for transparency are growing; everyone can expect to see 'everything' that is going on in an organisation and in society as a whole.

The digitalisation and democratisation of information has fast-forwarded this trend. And this is, of course, true both from a personal and a professional capacity. Most people are, on some level, constantly on display, on stage, online, visible. Personal and professional actions are seen and can have consequences. The line between the private and the professional person has become blurred. The expectation of transparency means that people want more openness and accessibility to the truth. This means transparency is also about managing and providing the truth.

What do they need?

Ultimately, it comes down to needing trust. Those external stakeholders need to be able to trust that an organisation is behaving ethically, keeping their promises and living up to expectations. And that trust is created through the experience touchpoints that connect the external world with an organisation. Employees are a major touchpoint and what they do, what they say, how they behave become a massive reality check on whether expectations are met or not. Employees are the ultimate 'brand ambassadors' who, together with the actual product or service, deliver on the brand promise or not.

A frustrated monologue

Samuel was on his way home from work. He was tired and annoyed as it had been a frustrating day of office politics and he felt as if he had achieved nothing all day.

He hailed a taxi outside the office and gave the driver instructions about where to take him. He then turned his attention to his phone and called his wife.

'Hi, can you talk? OK, great. It's been such a s**t day and I just needed to vent a bit. You know how I had prepared that presentation for our CIO? Well, as I expected, he didn't really listen to any of what I had to say. It's so typical for this

➤

company – people say they want something, but don't value it when they get it. It's all words. No one really walks the talk around here.' He paused.

'I am not the only person who has said this. We all think the leadership are not really telling us what is happening. It does not help me to do my job. I just get so frustrated.'

The taxi driver heard the monologue and grimaced to himself. This was not the first time he had heard this kind of expletive from employees of this company. He felt as if he and the other taxi drivers in town were experts at this company and all its failings. It was as if people forgot the driver was there, as if they assumed the driver was deaf or at least did not matter enough to consider what they were saying in front of him.

Well, I do not think I would choose to buy that company's products and services. I do not trust them – who would trust a company where employees talk so badly about it?

The company were a big employer in the town, so many of the taxi drivers were having the same experience and started talking amongst themselves. They were hearing all sorts of conversations and stories from people in their taxis. The bad-mouthing of the company was having an impact on the local community as well as the company (a well-known multinational company), who was dependent on a good standing, not least when it comes to attracting talent.

This short story highlights how every single person represents the company brand and, as such, is also a carrier of the company's reputation. Every person can have an impact on the world of external stakeholders and opinion makers.

When we live up to customers and other stakeholders' expectations, we strengthen the brand, we have a positive impact. When we do not live up to the expectations, we weaken the brand, we have a negative impact. The impact is on both stakeholders and brand. It, of course, affects personal brand, as how you represent the company is a reflection on your own brand too.

In Chapter 3, we talked about the importance of managing your own brand and reputation. In this chapter, we will take that a step further by reflecting on how you also have an impact on the organisational brand and reputation in how you interact with the external world of stakeholders and the public space.

Brand and reputation are linked but are not the same thing. Brand is about differentiation, a combination of design, products, services and communication that shape the brand promise and experience for customers – it is customer-focused. Reputation is how the organisation is perceived by the world around, how credible, responsible and trustworthy it is. Employees' behaviours impact both an organisation's reputation and how well the brand promise is kept.

Your impact is your legacy.

An organisation, just like individuals, teams and even countries, has a reputation. And that reputation is created over time, through words, actions and behaviours. But it is not set in stone – a reputation can quickly be tarnished and even ruined. A reputation should, most definitely, not be taken for granted. In fact, it should be taken very, very seriously. It can take us a long time: years, months, even decades, to build a strong, consistent and powerful one.

We can have a good, strong reputation, but only a few negative actions and behaviours that make others feel uncomfortable, disappointed or even betrayed can quickly damage that reputation and trust. And, once trust is damaged, it can take a long time to recover that trust. We all have our own reputation – in teams, individually or as an organisation. Whether we choose to work on it or not, we will have one. It is, therefore, highly relevant to ask: *What is our reputation? What do we want it to be? What does it need to be? This could and should be part of strategic leadership dialogues and considerations.*

A great reputation will sometimes travel ahead of us, and can open doors, just like a bad reputation can close doors.

If we ask you to think of a company right now that you are familiar with, you would have a view of them, right? You would have a view of their brand, their way of working, even the culture they create; what it is like to work there or what it is like to work with them. *It all comes down to the consistency in actions and behaviours, the promises kept and those relationships that have built the brand and reputation. When you think cars and safety, you may, for example, think of Volvo. When you think innovative design, you may think of Apple. When you think of a fun and creative place to work, you may think of Virgin, to mention a few well-known examples.*

Social media is a great way to keep in touch with clients, business partners and other stakeholders and can be an effective way to build interest and opinion, but needs to be carefully navigated. A comment, an imprint, can last forever. In that way, social media is very honest – we cannot erase our tracks. Even if a post or comment is deleted, it may already have been copied by someone and shared. On the other hand, if we are thoughtful and respectful about it, we should not have to. *Famous public figures tweeting is an example of this. Things said in the heat of the moment are creating ripples whose complete impact over time is hard to assess. They affect and create a reputation, good or bad. Some time for reflection and impulse-control is key when using social media.*

So, yes, reputation matters and should be taken seriously.

What organisational reputation are you creating right now? Take control of it. Think of how you, as a representative of your organisation, represent not just yourself but also your organisation when you engage with the world around you.

A story of impact: social media

In 2018, Uber's CEO crafted a sarcastic tweet,[24] calling Massachusetts Institute of Technology (MIT) 'Mathematically Incompetent Theories' in a response to an MIT study regarding the ride-sharing industry, which he clearly believed to be flawed or at least to contain misinterpreted data, hence disfavouring Uber. And MIT admitted later that there may have been a misinterpretation in response to Uber's chief economist's factual and measured response to the study, but the tweet from Uber's CEO was an unnecessary action that reflected badly on the organisation. This is also an example of how quickly hard work can be undone, as the CEO had worked hard at building a positive impression of Uber in the months ahead of the infamous tweet.

In the end, it may not have the most disastrous effect, but it can at least be seen as unnecessary. If nothing else, it is a reminder that we are all able to express whatever we like online, but it begs the question: do we really need to?

Solutions and tools

Here are some practical solutions and tools for having a positive impact on the external world of customers, partners, media and social media. The external world consists of your external stakeholders and they need to be thoughtfully handled. Create a stakeholder plan to plan for your engagement with them (see Chapter 4 for stakeholder planning).

A more extreme version of himself

While on holiday at a well-known ski resort, I stepped onto the balcony to take in the cold air and view the magnificent mountains covered in snow. On the balcony in the room next door, a well-known TV presenter was preparing to record to the camera crew. This person took a deep breath, pulled himself up taller and filled himself with energy. The camera started to roll. Smiling and enthusiastically, he spoke about this famous resort, telling the story of the slopes, the skiing, the views and the après ski. The presenter put himself into his media role. His voice changed, it was deeper and had more tonation in it, emphasising certain words for effect. He also ramped up his energy levels to be more energetic and animated. He was positive, smiling, making you feel engaged and wanting to hear more.

The TV presenter had put himself into a positive and energetic state.

When I met the presenter earlier in the day, he was quieter and more reserved. He changed his personality when filming to make an impact in front of the camera. He needed to be a more extreme version of himself to create impact at that time. He had the ability to be energetic and enthusiastic, but he just needed to increase the intensity, almost like 'turning up the volume' on himself to tap into his natural strength and use that to have more effect.

You can choose to have an impact too. What impact are you having right now? And what could you 'turn up'?

1. Choosing behaviours that make the difference

What kind of behaviours you demonstrate would either undermine or strengthen the brand and therefore create a negative or positive impact when you interact with external stakeholders and through the press and social media? Here are some examples. Use the empty boxes to fill in any other relevant behaviours in each of the categories that are important to you.

Behaviours for positive impact		Behaviours for negative impact	
Focused listening	Problem solving	Bad language	Disinterest
Showing respect	Sharing and using expertise	How criticism is handled	Not having enough knowledge
Taking the time	Quick handling of query/ request/ complaint	Not keeping promises	Sloppiness
Keeping promises	Taking an interest	Not having enough knowledge about the company, its external messages, promises, etc.	Being disrespectful
Showing empathy	Good manners	Lying	Arrogance
Understanding the customers' situation	How criticism is handled	Interrupting	Aggressiveness

When operating in the external world, as a representative not just for yourself but your organisation: *Which negative behaviours will you stop and which positive behaviours do/will you commit to? Which ones are particularly important in the context of your organisation's current reality?* List them below.

What I will *stop* doing	What I will *start* doing	What I will *continue* doing

2. Considering your impact on customers and their experience

We would, of course, be nowhere without our customers. We all need to keep delivering an experience that makes customers come back to us. Some companies ask their customers only one thing when collecting customer feedback – *would you recommend us to others?* And the answer to that question is straight-talking and highly relevant.

That is why being intentional about your customer impact is so interesting. It can be easy to overlook or underestimate your part in great customer experience. Everyone tends to be more important in this arena than they think. Think about what the customers want, need and expect and what role you play in that experience. Reflect on these questions to kick-start the process of intentional customer impact.

▌ What have your customers been promised and, therefore, what do they expect?

▌ What are they experiencing? Is there a gap between expectation and reality?

■ If you do not know, how could you find out what the customers experience? Could you listen in on customer calls? Read customer chats? What else could you do?

■ How (when/where) do you impact the customers' experience (even if through others)?

■ How do you live up to the brand promise?

■ How could you create excellent customer impact, experience? What could you do, specifically?

Surprise service

JR was on his way to the airport to catch a flight to Singapore. As he got to the airport, he realised that he had left his laptop behind. He tried to keep calm and called a friend with a key to his house and asked him if he could possibly get the bag for him and make a dash for the airport. Luckily, his friend answered and was close by so was able to support him in this. Time was tight, though, and JR hoped that traffic would not be an issue. He looked over to the security area and his heart sank as he saw the long queues – there was no way he would be able to wait out his friend and then join the long queues. He looked around and spotted the airline service desk and headed over there. He was met by a smiling woman who asked how she could help. He explained and she could see that he was trying to hide his stress.

'I can help,' she said. When do you think your friend will be here? And what's his name?

'He's called Pete and he should be here in 15 minutes, I hope.'

'OK. This is what we'll do. I'll wait for him by the entrance and you go and join the queue. I will come and find you either in the queue or by the gate. It will be OK.'

JR couldn't believe it, what service! He thanked her profusely and took off. Half an hour later, as he had just passed through

➤

security, she caught up with him and handed over the laptop with a smile.

JR nearly gave her a hug, that's how relieved he was. 'Thank you!' He exclaimed. 'I can't thank you enough!'

'My pleasure, sir. That's my job. I'm glad I could help.' And he could see that she meant it.

I'm flying this airline again, that's for sure, JR thought, as he hurried towards the gate.

3. Working effectively with your partners, suppliers, subcontractors, etc.

Great, collaborative impact makes you (and your organisation) someone others want to work with. How can you best create respectful, trustful relationships with suppliers, subcontractors and other external partners?

On the negative side: what if you are a poor payer? What if you regularly delay paying your suppliers on time because your cash flow is poor? What impact will that have on your supplier? How will they feel about you and your organisation?

On the positive side: what if you work creatively with your subcontractors, creating forums for innovative exchange and learning opportunities, discussing the latest trends, preparing for the future? What impact will that have on your supplier? How will they feel about you and your organisation?

It is obvious that everyone needs supportive external relationships and partnerships to succeed over time. Take a long-term view on your external stakeholders by answering the following questions.

▮ What industry trends can you see for the next 5–10 years? What will your organisation need to focus on?

▌ What new knowledge, skills, experience do those trends demand?

▌ Therefore, who do you need to partner with?

▌ How can you start identifying who those specific partners might be?

▌ How will you start building those needed relationships?

▌ Where could the people with whom I have relationships end up in the future or in their next role? My Boss, my customer, etc?

4. **Managing the media/press**

If it is your job to manage the media, then you will, of course, already be very familiar and comfortable with this. If it is not, take a moment to consider how you would represent your organisation should you be given the opportunity.

When talking to the press, you have to remember that you represent your company so whatever you say becomes what your company says, you become the 'official' spokesperson whether you intend to or not.

Here are some guidelines to use:-

▌ Be intentional – what do you want to say? Your messages could appear on a bill board or a make a headline, so think carefully about the message you want to portray. Think also about how what you say comes across: voice and physiology management matters. Think of your favourite TV reporter: their posture, facial expression, voice and energy contribute greatly to their impact. He/she can and does dial up and down these impact factors based on the story and situation.

▌ What are the three key messages that you want to portray during a conversation/interview? Stick to those three messages and, no matter what question you

are asked, ensure that you can connect one of those
messages into the answer.

▌ Keep your messages in line with the vision and values.
Ensure you are relating everything back to the bigger
purpose, giving them the big *why: Why we are doing
this, in line with our purpose?*

▌ Think of the 'red thread'. This means make all the
connections from the subject or discussion you are
having to the vision and the bigger purpose. Help them to
connect the red thread from the discussion to the bigger
vision. Make the links and connections visible and clear.

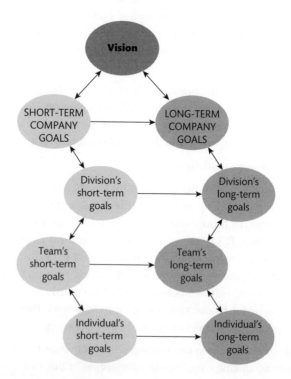

The red thread

▌ Ensure you 'label' what you say and link it to the business and show them the threads and connections.

Practise by doing this exercise. Take a message you need to communicate. Now, what are the three key messages you want to get across? Practise asking yourself or ask a colleague to help by asking questions and then answering by using one of your three messages. Practise making the links and weaving the conversation back to your points, no matter what questions are asked.

The circus is in town

A senior leader of a large multinational organisation was being interviewed by a local radio station. The organisation was very well known in the local area and employed a large number of people in the community. The organisation had decided to sponsor a state circus that was arriving in the town for a few weeks. The radio presenter asked many questions about why this large company would sponsor a circus. The leader had the three key messages ready and kept answering the question by saying that this organisation was very pleased to be active in the local community and support this activity as it was a way of getting people together to see a spectacle of different skills.

The leader kept reiterating the organisation was active in the local community as an important employer in the area. The radio presenter then started to probe, even saying that the circus is a cruel place and that keeping animals was controversial. (It was a state circus with no animals so a rather pointless questioning by the presenter but they were trying to provoke the leader to make more of a sensational story). The leader kept coming back to the three key messages and stayed on track, not being influenced by the presenter's change of tack.

5. Social media and brand management

Think of yourself as *one* online person. It does not matter if you are acting in your personal or your professional life; if it is going on online, it could be seen by more people than those intended. You may not be able to dictate this for others (unless you have specific organisational social media conduct codes in place) but you can always take responsibility for your own social media activities and messages and what you role model for those around you.

Unless you work in politics, be careful with how you comment on political issues as this can quickly turn into slinging matches, which can backfire into the workspace.

Think of yourself as your own, your team's, your organisation's brand ambassador. *Without a good, strong reputation, it is hard to get others to trust you and work with you – which, in turn, makes it hard to deliver great results.*

Here are five quick reflection exercises to review and manage a strong, positive, consistent brand and reputation online:

▌ What does your organisation want to be known for, what do you want others to see about you? That you are collaborative, responsible, knowledgeable? Or something else? Whatever it is, engage your team in discussion and agreement on how to achieve that, keeping in mind that reputation is greatly influenced by how you do something, not just what you do. It needs to be authentic.

▌ What messages do you want to put out there? Are there any key words that should be used? Should you share research, industry data, new products and services? Should you engage with customers, potential customers, other stakeholders?

▌ When actively interacting with others online, take responsibility, not just for your actions, but maybe, even more importantly, your *reactions.* Do not let responses become automatic; use the moment between trigger and response to carefully choose how you will respond to the words and actions of others. Every moment counts. Think about how your response will impact the other party and how it will influence their perception of you and the organisation.

▌ What professional social media apps are you using? What is your LinkedIn profile looking like? Do you have a representative photo? Is there enough information about what you do and how you represent your organisation? Add depth and personality to your profile by asking for recommendations and endorsements.

▌ What personal social media apps are you using? What are you sharing there? Would you be happy for anyone to see that? Are you on Twitter? If so, even if you put an 'Opinions are my own' caption, this may not be enough to fully manage the impact you have and how it reflects on the organisation you work for. This is especially true when you are a leader – you always represent the company you work for and your actions are not just seen by external audiences but also internal ones.

Voices of impact

Impact is the feeling and response we create in others.

Here are some examples linked to this chapter of how an action or behaviour impacts people's feelings and, therefore, how they respond at work. This is how impact sounds and feels. They clearly show that what we do has consequences, good or bad. This gives us a greater understanding that we have the ability to affect our outcomes every moment of every day. This is a big responsibility and, as a leader, it is magnified through the wide sphere of influence that comes with a leadership role.

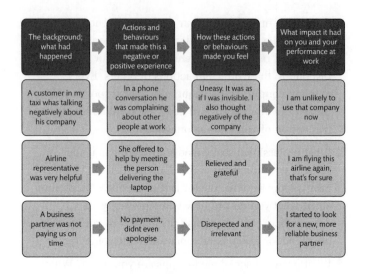

The background; what had happened	Actions and behaviours that made this a negative or positive experience	How these actions or behaviours made you feel	What impact it had on you and your performance at work
A customer in my taxi whas talking negatively about his company	In a phone conversation he was complaining about other people at work	Uneasy. It was as if I was invisible. I also thought negatively of the company	I am unlikely to use that company now
Airline representative was very helpful	She offered to help by meeting the person delivering the laptop	Relieved and grateful	I am flying this airline again, that's for sure
A business partner was not paying us on time	No payment, didnt even apologise	Disrepected and irrelevant	I started to look for a new, more reliable business partner

More solutions: the role your own thoughts, feelings and behaviours play

When wanting to take control over your impact on the external world, you first need to impact yourself.

> **What we think affects how we feel, and how we feel affects how we think.**

You can actively replace thoughts and feelings that are counterproductive to positive impact.

It is estimated[25] that a person experiences up to as many as 70,000 thoughts per day.

Many of those thoughts are habits that affect a person's mindset or outlook and, therefore, the impact they have on the world around them. It starts from within.

On the next page are some examples of negative thoughts, their impact on feelings and how they can be changed to new constructive thoughts to drive more effective impact behaviour.

Negative thought	Negative feeling	Ineffective behaviour	Constructive thought	Constructive feeling	Effective behaviour
I don't trust him!	Aversion	Avoiding the person and the issue	He's doing his best and I can play my part in creating trust	Confidence	Listening and interacting with an open mind
She is wrong!	Anger	Engaging in word wars online	It's OK that she has a different opinion, I don't need to get involved	Self-control, calm	Choosing to step back and carefully choosing how to engage online
Stupid questioning by reporter about the circus (with no animals!)	Feeling at risk of being manipulated	Snappy, sharp response to reporter	She's just doing her job	Calm understanding	Taking time to choose a response, building a good relationship for next time

Summary

The external world is immense and could include many more current and future stakeholders than described here. Regardless, the main point is that the ripple effect of people's behaviour when multiplied in the external world is enormous. We all need to be aware of how the waves of impact that are created through an increasingly transparent reality have an impact on the world around. Even if we wanted to, we cannot *not* have an impact. The world becomes more and more interconnected and external stakeholder management deserves a serious place in any leader's agenda and work priorities.

THE EFFECT ON CULTURE

The internal culture of an organisation plays a large role in how the organisation is perceived in the external world. What happens inside the culture with employees permeates to the outside world of stakeholders. The culture is always on display. Culture is the behaviours, beliefs, assumptions, values and ways of interacting that differentiate one organisation from another. Whether you know what it is or not, you *have* a culture and it is on display. So, by paying attention to and thinking about your impact externally, how you are a brand ambassador, you reinforce that strong culture internally too.

Self-assessment

After you have implemented the solutions in this chapter, answer these questions again to see the progress you have made.

How would you rate your ability to create impact on the external world in these areas?

	1 Very poor	2 Poor	3 Just OK	4 Good	5 Excellent
Choosing behaviours that make the difference					
Considering your impact on customers and their experience					
Working effectively with your partners, suppliers, subcontractors, etc.					
Managing the media/press					
Social media and brand management					

It takes many good deeds to build a good reputation and only one bad one to lose it.

Benjamin Franklin

Impact for different desired outcomes

S ometimes, business strategies and desired outcomes can and should be considered from a different impact perspective. This part of the book helps you think through the approach to take in order to achieve said outcome, which goes beyond a tactical project plan – it guides you through who will be impacted by the outcome, in which way and how to communicate along the way.

Each chapter provides an Impact Road Map to work through to create a Game Plan, helping you achieve each specific outcome. There are tools and tips included in all steps to help you move forward.

8

Collaborative impact

Self-assessment

Before reading this chapter, do the following quick self-assessment.

How would you rate your ability to create collaborative impact in these areas:-

	1 Very poor	2 Poor	3 Just OK	4 Good	5 Excellent
Helping people to know each other better to aid open communication					
Making it easy for people to share information, knowledge and ideas					
Resolving conflict and tension					

The case for collaboration

The speed of change that we are experiencing in society today means that most, if not all, organisations will sooner or later either disrupt *or* be disrupted by old or new players in the market. *To disrupt* is to achieve disruptive innovation, to do something that radically changes the status quo, and no one can do this on their own.

This kind of disruption demands a 'new' kind of leadership: leaders who can navigate, lead and collaborate through the choppy waters of constant change. It demands some serious collaboration.

To collaborate is a bit like bringing all the pieces together in a jigsaw. They can all fit together perfectly and, if a piece is missing, the picture will be incomplete. Everyone brings their unique piece to the jigsaw at work, and leaders do well to recognise the value of bringing all the pieces together.

Collaboration, then, is combining:

▌ hearts and minds

▌ skills and traits

▌ knowledge and wisdom

▌ strengths and diversity

▌ support and help

▌ actions and commitment

The ability to share and combine all of those components is what you're driving for when wanting to have a collaborative impact. You want to make it appealing and easy for people to collaborate. People's habits at work form the culture, which makes actions and behaviours almost automatic. To be collaborative, therefore, you need to have a culture of learning. To learn is to not need to be right, to be open to learning from others and recognising that you can achieve more that way than you would do alone. That is a collaborative culture of learning. We are intentionally saying this again – *it starts with you* – what you do is contagious. *Are you role modelling collaboration and learning?*

You also need to be aware that conflict and tension between people that do not get properly resolved create stress, thereby impacting both mental/emotional and physical health, hence hindering collaboration. For that reason, conflict management is a key skill for both leaders and team members that want to be part of a healthy, productive and collaborative team experience. In fact, we should call this conflict leadership not just management. All of us need to *lead* through conflict, rather than just reactively respond to it when it happens. Leadership, after all, is the act of influencing others and we all need to influence each other to constructively resolve conflict and use the creative power of the difference of opinion. It is everyone's responsibility.

Conflict and tension between people can have many different causes and can play itself out in many varied forms. Sometimes, it can be an open, argumentative conflict and, sometimes, it can be in a passive aggressive form, where it is less obvious and, therefore, more difficult to address.

These are the most common reasons for conflict and a reluctance to collaborate that we regularly observe between people at work:

- Lack of effective communication, leading to rumour mills that erode trust
- Personal differences, where people do not understand each other and/or do not like each other and think in terms of 'I'm right, you're wrong'
- Conflicting goals and priorities, particularly common in matrix environments
- Being geograpichally dispersed, not having easy access to each other
- Competitive behaviours, driven by factors such as unclear roles and responsibilities

The negative impact of conflict

If conflict and tension are not managed or, more importantly, led, they erode trust and make people work on their own rather than collaborate with others. In really bad cases, it also makes people work against each other, which is both stressful and unproductive. Considering how much time most people spend at work, this is not how they want to spend their time feeling, not to mention the productivity drain and cost implications.

Conflict is not a bad thing per se

It is simply a difference of opinion. An opinion in and of itself is neither good nor bad. It is the interpretation that we make that can create a negative sense of conflict, which adversely impacts collaboration.

Conflict arises from the idea that something is either right or wrong, which, in turn, means that when opinions differ someone is either right or wrong. When people think like that, they want to be right and then they no longer look for the potential value in the other person's view. And, if both parties want to be right, tension is then created by both of them not feeling listened to or valued – and the sense of tension and conflict grows.

Collaborative impact is about getting people to collaborate willingly and proactively. When this happens, you effectively shape a collaborative culture – 'how things get done around here'. In many organisations, people are not located in the same place and are part of a matrix, reporting to multiple leaders. This requires greater emphasis on collaboration to make it a reality. It is less likely to happen by chance, it needs to be done with intention. A recent study[27] shows that organisations that promote collaboration were five times more likely to be high performing.

On average, we spend 37 hours a week at work, which means that most of us spend more time with our colleagues than with our family and friends. And, if things are not amicable with the people we work with or our teams do not collaborate efficiently, those 37 hours are going to be painful.

Let us reflect on and create a Road Map for how to achieve collaborative impact. These steps include tools and tips to achieve your outcome.

The collaborative impact Roadmap

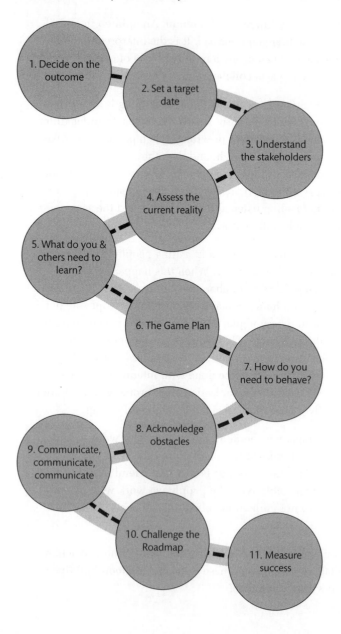

Roadmap step 1: decide on the outcome

So, what is it that you want to achieve? For what purpose do you want people to collaborate better, more effectively? The clearer you can be on this, the more pull it will have on you and the people involved, helping you make choices to move you towards it. Part of that thought process could involve those you want to get to collaborate better.

One important aspect of collaboration is focusing on the relationships that are crucial for long-term success. This could be clients, suppliers, potential clients and colleagues, to mention a few. By investing time on being respectful and collaborative *now,* you can create a respectful and collaborative relationship over time. This is not just the 'right thing' to do, but it will also make it easier to get them to want to work with you in the future. And, with great relationships also come recommendations; clients and stakeholders that seek you out because they have seen your consistent, respectful and collaborative approach over time.

Ultimately, collaborative focus is about being strategic, to consider the effects of actions, to decide what steps to take next. Great teams think about how to work together – in order to maximise the value given to customers and the organisation. Collaboration can be the differentiator when it comes to promotion too. When moving up the career ladder and going for another job, the candidate that shows they are great at collaborating will stand out. So, the more you can encourage and develop high-level collaboration, the more *everyone* will benefit. The more senior you are, the more overview you have of collaborative opportunities between people, so you may need to be the instigator of it.

So what could an outcome look like? Let us use an example. We will continue using this example throughout the chapter.

Stephen's results had always been really good. The last few months they had started to dip, and they were no longer achieving their monthly targets. Helmut was consistently on his case, asking him what he was doing about it and why there was a change in the numbers.

There had been a number of changes in the team, some structural changes as well and changes from the headquarters. This was making it more challenging for people to see what role they played, so they all just got their head down and did their own thing. Interaction reduced and collaboration suffered. Stephen was trying very hard, but nothing was happening.

Stephen decided he wanted them to collaborate again, recognising that this was the only way they could deliver the results. It was obvious to him. At the next quarterly reporting, Stephen had to demonstrate an improvement.

To make sense, any outcome should contribute to the overall vision and purpose of the organisation. There needs be a red thread from the outcome you identify to each person's part in it.

There has to be a compelling reason to drive collaboration, rather than just 'it's the nice thing to do'. And, in this particular case, there is also a burning platform – they are expected to deliver on their goals, period.

> The outcome in this case can be described as 'For our team to deliver our monthly targets by actively working together, sharing our knowledge, insights and creative thinking.'

Fill in your collaborative outcome below – why you want people to collaborate better, more effectively.

> My collaborative outcome is:

Roadmap step 2: set a target date

By when do you want to achieve this? And, if there is not an obvious target date, do you need to create one? Deadlines focus the mind and start an internal clock ticking. Without a clear endpoint, things can drift and procrastination can kick in. What gets measured gets done.

> In this chapter's story, Stephen has given himself three months to turn this situation around.

What is your target date? Fill it in here.

> The target date is:

Roadmap step 3: understand the stakeholders

Who does this involve and impact? Who are your stakeholders? What do you know and understand about them? What more do you need to know about them?

Stephen had thought he knew his team members quite well, but this recent shift in behaviours has made him realise that he is missing something and that he needs to get more involved to figure out what is going on. Stephen recognises that the changes in structure have affected people more than he had anticipated. He knows his team normally want to do well and take pride in their work and, therefore, he needs to use that drive and pride to help them concentrate on solving this. Stephen plans to use that team strength as a lever for the development he wants to achieve.

Stephen is also painfully aware that there are other stakeholders involved. Now that the team is not performing, more interest and pressure are coming from other senior leaders, as well as Helmut. The reason for the increased interest is linked to the recent structural changes, which have created new matrix dependencies and a higher demand for transparency.

Stephen now recognises he can no longer overlook this new group of stakeholders. He decides to do some research into the various players' agendas, priorities and goals.

Stephen wants his team members to work better together, so his collaborative impact is aimed at them. However, the other senior stakeholders have expectations that need to be met so Stephen also needs to manage them carefully at the same time. This is not an additional thing to do, *it is the job* for Stephen. So many leaders see this as an additional task when it is the job of the leader to be influencing and impacting the stakeholders along the way.

As Stephen is working out his stakeholders, when he has taken the time to stop and reflect on the bigger picture, he realises there are several stakeholder groups to balance, as well as his team members. He identifies them as: his team, his peers and their teams, Helmut, Helmut's peers – and he decides to talk to Helmut as well as to his own peers to get clarity on their priorities and expectations so that he can complete the stakeholder analysis. Stephen increases his chances of the best possible stakeholder impact, which would not have happened had he not taken the time for reflection.

You must stop and reflect on the bigger picture, be strategic and consider each stakeholder individually as well as how they impact each other.

Please complete your own stakeholder analysis below.

My stakeholders are:

This is what I know about them and their needs:

For more in-depth information on stakeholder planning, please go to Chapter 4.

Roadmap step 4: assess the current reality

Be realistic about where you currently are with regards to collaboration for this specific outcome. Notice the difference between where you are right now and where you want to be (your outcome). How big is the gap? You really need to get a sense of how big or small the gap is so that you can make a realistic assessment of what it will take to close the gap. Do not be judgemental about it, accept the current reality as it is – it is not good, bad, right or wrong.

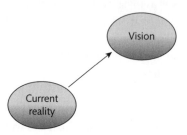

Whenever there is a gap between how things are now and how you want them to be, there is a natural tension that is created in that space. That tension can be described as an elastic band pulled taut between the current and future situation. Unless the desired outcome is strong enough to pull you out of the current reality, you will default back into current reality. So make sure the outcome you are after is very clear and shared with those whom it concerns.

Stephen was observing his team on a call. Sophia seemed distant and not really engaged, as she had always been previously. Samuel had the answers to the questions being asked but chose to keep that information to himself. JR was dominating the meeting, talking at people rather than having a dialogue. He was in 'transmit mode', rather than 'receive'.

Blame was being put on other teams and individuals for the issues they were experiencing.

In contemplating the current situation, Stephen got frustrated with what he was experiencing. This minimal collaboration was far from the generous collaboration he expected of his team and it was important for him to close that gap.

> In their current reality, they were not listening to each other, they were withholding information; some team members were dominating the meeting.

What does your current reality look like (in contrast to your outcome)? Write it down here.

> Our current reality looks like this:

What are you going to do with that distance, that natural tension that is created between the current reality and the desired outcome? Hold on to any ideas you are having – we will get to action planning in step 6.

Roadmap step 5: what do you and others need to learn?

What do you need to learn (about) to be able to do this? What do your stakeholders need to learn?

Collaborating efficiently requires us to want to learn and to operate in a learning culture. At this pace of change, we cannot possibly know it all. We need to be a 'learn it all' rather than a 'know it all', so think hard about what you and others need to learn.

Teamwork had been quite easy before, when they were working in a familiar, comfortable structure. Then it had been easy to talk about how to work together. Now everyone was tip-toeing around, not quite knowing how things were supposed to work. Were there any overlaps and how would they all be able to communicate and collaborate when they were not all in the same location? Especially if they did not all have completely aligned goals and, maybe, even conflicting priorities.

Christine was disappointed about not getting a possible promotion, Anna now had a dotted reporting line into a person she did not like much and also did not trust. And they all seemed to have more attention from Helmut than they were used to and that was not helping with the hesitant behaviours that were on display.

Stephen needs to get into the depths of what is actually causing the problem. He has to recognise the impact the structural changes have had on his team, and learn how to make that impact more positive. He also wants to learn more about managing his boss Helmut because his boss is interfering, so Stephen needs to influence Helmut to be a more constructive party in this change. He needs to learn how to give more context and share the reality of how this change has impacted his team when he talks to Helmut. Helmut needs to learn more about the team, and the team needs to learn to operate in a more matrixed environment.

What learnings are needed for you and your stakeholders? Capture your observations in the box on the next page.

This is what I need to learn about:

This is what my stakeholders need to learn about:

Roadmap step 6: the Game Plan

What needs doing?
Who will do it?
When will it be done?

As you bring together all your thoughts and ideas for how to get people to collaborate for this specific outcome, remember that they may need to be made aware of the burning reason to collaborate. They need to see their own impact on each other and how that has an effect on the level of collaboration that can happen.

In our book *The Team Formula: A Leadership Tale of a Team Who Found Their Way,*[28] we outlined the formula to effective, collaborative teams.

Reflect on these factors to identify the areas that would be relevant for you to focus on in your Game Plan.

1. **Get together as a team.** Make a conscious decision to create a collaborative team. Take the time to do it, plan it (as it rarely happens by chance).

2. **Get to know each other much deeper, creating trust.** Everyone is different and people usually do the best they can and rarely intend to annoy others or create

conflict. Just because someone does not think or feel like you, they do not have to be wrong. So, if you get annoyed with someone, assume that they are acting with positive intention and notice the difference in your own reaction. Take a moment and think about what difference it would make if we all assumed positive intent. *It feels different, right?*

3. **Really talk to each other openly, be courageous.** There can never be too much communication. Communicate even when you have nothing to say, especially in times of change. Provide the transparency that makes people feel informed and at ease, so they can focus on the job rather than what they think is not being communicated. Be a transparency role model. Healthy debate can be created if you voice disagreement in a good way. Voicing the disagreement is the key, to just take that first step and talk about it – while assuming positive intent and looking for the right outcome and, of course, letting go of the need to be right.

4. **Give each other behavioural TOP feedback.** Encourage peer-to-peer coaching, where team/matrix members share their observations in a factual, supportive way – highlighting behaviours observed, impact created and suggestions for the future. For more information on the TOP feedback model, please go to Chapter 5.

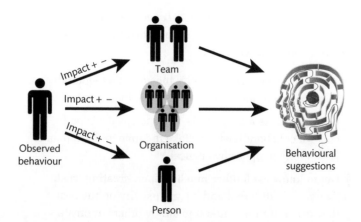

▌ **Build on individual and team strengths, creating drive and self-esteem.** No one is best at everything, everyone is best at something. Identify all the strengths that team/matrix members have and have a dialogue about how to make the most of them for the benefit of all.

▌ **Agree on your team purpose and direction.** Identify shared or at least aligned, non-conflicting, goals. Think strategically with a short-, medium- and long-term focus. Link goals to purpose and company vision. Make sure that team/matrix members' individual goals are linked to each other's and to the overall goals of the team. With connected goals, team members have a stake in each other's success and are encouraged to work together to achieve results. Sometimes, you may need to help people to see the links between what they do and what the others do and how they are dependent on each other. Make the links to goals explicit; do not just expect team members to see them automatically.

▌ **Decide how to work together and how to measure success.** Have clear roles and responsibilities that eliminate overlaps and rework. Ensure the creation of and buy-in to effective work processes and tools that aid communication and collaboration.

▌ **Be generous: fearlessly share what you know with your colleagues.** When everyone acts with generosity, recognising that knowledge breeds new knowledge when shared, true creative dialogues take place and new, innovative solutions can be found. This is the epitomy of powerful collaboration – together everyone achieves more.

▌ **Commit to what has been agreed together.** Create a commitment document, a team agreement, that everyone signs and keep it somewhere online or physically, where everyone can see it. The process of signing something together further cements the importance of the commitment.

▌ **Keep your promise, hold each other accountable.**
Unless kept, promises quickly erode trust and any
willingness to collaborate. Promises tend to be stronger
than commitments, and they tend to be more personal
and are made at an individual level. Both breaking and
keeping a promise impacts at an emotional level.

From previous experience, Stephen had learnt that there are
pretty much two main ways to lead a team. The first option is
letting people get on with their jobs individually with very little
'team' interaction or guidance from the leader. The second way
is being a proactive leader, providing the team with the direction,
structure and culture that can allow it to be a great team.

Having led a team through the second option before, he
reflected on how any change a team goes through tends to
require some additional focus. This helps get the team focused
on the shared purpose and how that is best fulfilled together.
He knows so well that getting a team to work well together
requires work up front, and that is what he needs to do now.

Leaders rarely feel they have the time to truly focus on
developing effective teams, particularly if they are going
through a time-consuming change process, but it is definitely
an investment that pays off, and more quickly than you would
think. If you can get your team fully aligned, working well
together, you will be able to deliver better results more quickly.

Stephen decides to reconnect the team's goals, engaging the
team in dialogue about how to best achieve them. He plans to
give more specific feedback to team members on how they are
working now compared to how they have done before, and the
impact of that. He needs to deal with any conflict and tension that
have been created by the changes in organisational structure and
help the team/matrix members see the possibilities more clearly.

Complete your Game Plan below.

What to do	How to do it	Who will do it	When to get it done	What impact will this have on collaboration?

Roadmap step 7: how do you need to behave?

How do you need to behave? How will those behaviours make others feel so that they want to collaborate more?

Here are a few factors to consider.

You, of course, need to be collaborative yourself – behaviours are contagious. Do what you ask others to do. It starts with you. What are you role modelling?

The solutions you have identifed in your Game Plan work best when carried out with supporting 'how to' behaviours. The actions on their own will take you so far. With the right behaviours, you walk the talk and your collaborative impact is greater.

As mentioned in the previous step, collaboration is easier and more straightforward if there is a shared purpose, a reason for being. This may need to be reiterated; people need to be reminded through continuous communication.

As collaboration is often hindered by conflict, your conflict leadership behaviours are key. Here are some additional behaviours that are critical when 'leading conflict' and building trust, when fostering collaboration:

- Be accepting (of self and others)
- Be curious
- Be respectful
- Be genuinely interested in people
- Be generous, share what you know
- Give credit when it is due
- Let go of the need to 'be right'
- Keep your promises (be trustworthy)

Stephen noticed in himself he was getting impacted by the team's frustration. He was becoming stressed and this was not a good place to be for him. Like everyone else, he is not at his best when stressed, he is less mentally and emotionally resourceful and not able to access his clear thinking, insights and wisdom. He is just not the best version of himself.

His habit of journalling made him reflect on his own actions and reactions and he knew he had to think very carefully about his own behaviours, not just for his team but for himself. He needed to see to his own behaviours first, to then help his team members come around again and return to greater and more extensive collaboration.

Stephen needs to give more direction, be involved, be more collaborative himself, show he is inspiring and instil hope and excitement around the new way of working. He can choose to tap into his inspiring style and to have patience and not let himself be dragged into the frustrations of others. He *does* have a choice.

So, how do you choose to behave to drive collaboration?

This is how I choose to behave	This is how each of these behaviours will have an impact on the steps of my Game Plan

Roadmap step 8: acknowledge obstacles

What obstacles are there? Or could there be? How can they be overcome?

Common obstacles to teamwork are:

- personality differences
- not enough trust
- not seeing the relevance or importance of working together
- first (negative) impressions last
- egos get in the way
- lack of time
- people being too busy
- people's mindsets
- reluctance to share information/experience
- geographical distance

These can all lead to hesitancy or unwillingness to collaborate, which makes it hard to perform even the simplest of tasks.

With the team in six different locations and three different time zones, it had so far been hard to find a great way of communicating effectively, especially as they did not all know each other so it was not so easy to just pick up the phone and talk. On top of that, everyone was so busy so they did not prioritise reaching out or actively collaborating.

Stephen feels like he has to have all the answers. He is finding it hard to ask for help. He is also very busy and finding it difficult to choose to set time aside. On reflection, he also realised that he would like to involve the team in solutions for how to communicate effectively despite the geographical divide.

What obstacles do you see that need overcoming – for you, the team(s), the organisation?

The obstacles I can foresee:

How I will overcome them:

Roadmap step 9: communicate, communicate, communicate

What will you communicate? Who, when, how, to whom?
How do you need to be and behave in your communication?

When thinking about communication for a specific outcome, often there are two aspects of two-way communication that need particular attention.

The first one is *framing* – how will you frame the message overall, particularly when you first share it? Framing is very much about how you communicate, the words you use, the stories you tell, the way you help people see the importance in what you are saying. It is about communicating a message in such a way that you influence people to listen to you. How are you building in a feedback loop so you can get immediate input from those involved?

The second one is the structure and determination of ongoing progress and results communication needed to keep people motivated and help them see the progress made. This would, typically, involve frequency, method, channel and feedback loop.

As the team members are working more independently than before, Stephen knows he needs to ramp up communication, to help the team/matrix move through the changes more quickly. He also plans to take greater charge of his senior stakeholder communication, to meet their expectations.

Stephen identifies the following key messages that his various stakeholders will benefit from hearing and being reminded of.

His team:

▌ This is our shared purpose/goal.

▌ Together we can achieve more.

▌ This is how I will support you.

▌ Creative dialogue is never done alone.

His boss Helmut:

▌ This is what I'm doing to . . .

▌ This is how we will support you.

▌ My team needs your support in the following way . . .

Other senior leaders:

▌ This is where we are right now.

▌ This is the progress we have made.

▌ This is how we can support you.

▌ This is what you could do to support in your area.

What do you want your stakeholders to hear? Fill in the speech bubbles below.

Roadmap step 10: challenge the Roadmap

Challenge your draft Impact Roadmap – how could you think of all of this differently?

OK, let us question everything one more time. What if there was another way to achieve this collaborative outcome? Review what you have reflected on so far and ask yourself – how could I think of all this differently? Could there be a completely different approach to get people to collaborate effectively?

Leave it for a day and review again	Ask a friend!
Talk to a peer	Talk to your team

Look at it from a new perspective by imagining yourself as someone else–a few examples below (imagine how they would look and sound)–what would they do?
Elvis Presley
Your son/daughter
J. K. Rowling
Or someone else!

Or are there any additional ideas that you want to add to your plan so far?

When challenging my current thinking, this is what I come up with:

Roadmap step 11: measure the success

How are you going to measure your collaborative outcome? How will you know if you have achieved the level of collaboration you were aiming for? How will you ensure you follow through and follow up on your way to achieving the outcome? And how will you celebrate the success?

The team are having a review of how things are going, what has worked and what has not. Have they achieved their targets? This is something Stephen is choosing to do with the team each month now rather than just at the end of the three months.

Stephen knows collaboration will, ultimately, show in his team's results. And it will show in how people feel about being at work. For that reason, he chooses two main measures – overall goal achievement and internal and external team feedback. He chooses to celebrate by taking his team out for dinner.

How will you make sure you follow through and measure and celebrate success?

This is how I will follow through and follow up:

This is how I will measure success:

This is how I will celebrate success:

THE EFFECT ON CULTURE

If you want to create a culture of collaboration, you may want to create a culture of learning too. To learn is not the need to be right, it is to be open to learning from others. That is a collaborative culture of learning. Be aware of what you are rewarding, and ensure you are rewarding team and collaborative behaviour. Be explicit and say *why* you are rewarding that positive behaviour and notice how true collaboration starts to become the cultural norm.

Now that you have worked your way through how you will lead in order to achieve collaborative impact, you may also want to transfer your notes and create a complete plan by filling in the Impact Roadmap Worksheet at the back of the book or by downloading it from www.2020visionleader.com/ImpactRoadmap.

Self-assessment

Now that you have created your Impact Roadmap, please review
the progress you have made by completing this self-assessment.

How would you rate your ability to create collaborative impact in
these areas:

	1 Very poor	2 Poor	3 Just OK	4 Good	5 Excellent
Helping people to know each other better to aid open communication					
Making it easy for people to share information, knowledge and ideas					
Resolving conflict and tension					

The secret is to gang up on the problem, rather than each other.

Thomas Stallkamp

9 Change-driving impact

LEADERSHIP FACT

Did you know?

Organisations with better financial performance have more women in leadership roles.[29]

Self-assessment

Before reading this chapter, do the following quick self-assessment.

How would you rate your ability to create change-driving impact in these areas?

	1 Very poor	2 Poor	3 Just OK	4 Good	5 Excellent
Helping people to embrace change					
Getting people to help drive change					
Allowing people to work together to create change					

The case for embracing and driving change

Successful change needs everyone onboard. This chapter explores and outlines how you can plan your impact to achieve successful change, by helping people embrace it and help drive it.

We have learned that people will change for one of two reasons:-

▌ **A burning platform.** When there is something that has to be done or there are consequences if it is not. When the current reality is so painful that people need to move away from it.

▌ **A compelling reason.** When there is something they strongly desire that pulls them towards it.

A strong allegiance

During the merger of the two companies, Samuel felt a strong allegiance with his old brand; he wanted to hold onto the good things that they had created. He liked what they stood for. Stephen was keen to see the merger progress. He was happy to see that there was change ahead and was keen for the new ideas that would be spilling into the newly merged company.

These feelings can create two camps, often pulling people in different directions. Some pull away from what they feel is painful with the new company and others feel it is a pleasure to be working in a new environment and are excited by the change. It is extra important in those scenarios to quickly get teams together to explore their new joint purpose and direction. Otherwise, the divide will be allowed to grow and it can take longer to get the organisation off to a new start. It is better to create that shared feeling and excitement about something new, including taking what was good in the old brand, not losing that, while adding to the new brand. This approach ensures there is value being added to the merger. After all that is the reason for it in the first place!

By keeping these two reasons in mind, you can work out how best to motivate and inspire people to change. Being aware of the real reason for change helps you to map out your approach. Is it moving towards something compelling or away from something that is more painful?

For years, managing change has been a key necessity for organisations across the globe.

Managing change is largely a reactive response to changes that occur, in order to make those changes work. Being able to manage change ensures your business can effectively handle the circumstances brought on by internal and external events.

But simply managing change is not enough to make the most of opportunities on the horizon; we also need to be able to lead change.

So, should we be adding 'change leadership' to our vocabulary, alongside 'change management'? Definitely!

Change leadership, not just change management.

What does change leadership involve?

Be proactive

To lead change is to be proactive. It is thinking ahead: *What do we need to do next, how do we need to change to be able to meet customers'/the world's needs to be successful?* It is looking around you: *What's going on in the market, the world and the society I'm in? What do I need to be aware of? What are the signs that things might be changing or that they should change?*

Be strategic

Why are we changing? How will it contribute to the vision? What is the red thread, what are the links that connect me and everyone else to each other and to the overall vision?

Take control

To lead change is to take control, which is a much better place to be in than feeling out of control. When you start to be proactive about change, you make it a very natural thing and, potentially, less threatening to your team members.

Involve your team

Another key aspect of leading change is to involve employees *in* it. It is not just the role of the leader to lead change. All employees can actively scan the world around them to understand the bigger picture and make better decisions for the organisation.

The emotional reaction to change – be aware of your and others' emotions

Change is inherently emotional. Understand what it does to you, the emotional reaction that you have and how that is leaking to others. Others, on the other hand, may be having a different emotional reaction. A huge part of dealing with change is understanding how you are reacting with others and how they are reacting.

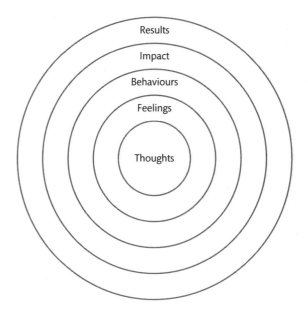

The (2020 Vision) Leader Impact Model™

How people feel impacts how connected they are to the change and, therefore, if the change actually occurs. This is the reason that many changes fail, because the emotional aspects have been ignored. Many people want to ignore the emotional phase of change as it is the hardest to deal with. Others are aware of the emotional phase but want to quickly skip over it.

This describes the ripple effect of leading and managing your inner self, which is illustrated in the model above.

This model shows how the thoughts we have will impact our feelings, which then make us behave in a certain way in line with our feelings. This results in how we impact others and, therefore, the results that we start to get.

WIIFM? What's in it for me?

As the merger became a reality, Helmut had reflected on what resources he needed in place in order to progress the expected growth as quickly as possible. His direct report Samuel had, so far, done a good job as the leader of one of his key teams, but Helmut did not think he was agile enough in his thinking and, therefore, decided to demote Samuel and put Stephen in his place instead, effectively as Samuel's manager.

As soon as Helmut had made the decision, he proceeded to approach Stephen, offering him the new role. Stephen happily accepted but was not immediately made aware that Samuel would still be around, now as his direct report. Two days before Stephen was about to join the team, Helmut decided to tell Samuel about his demotion and he did so without much consideration for how Samuel would react. Samuel was shocked and angry and felt that he had been very unfairly treated. At the same time, he did not want to have to find a new job so he decided that, as he would get to keep his salary, he would stay around – but his heart was not in it any more and he was not going to make Stephen's life easy.

In this example, Samuel reacted to change with the first thoughts of WIIFM. It is a natural human reaction that cannot be ignored and needs to be taken into consideration. This was not a good situation for anyone and, although Helmut had spent time thinking about the changes he was going to make, he had not thought about the impact on his team members.

During any change, people will ask themselves: *What is in it for me? How does it affect me? What does it mean for me, my work, my life, my family, home?*

Remember that people are convinced in different ways, so you will need to use different methods to engage them in the change; it cannot always be one size fits all.

Change leadership involves thinking of all the dynamics detailed above. When dealing with change, here are the biggest change scenarios we see people come up against regularly:

- mergers, acquisitions and de-mergers
- change of leader
- digital transformation, including automation, artificial intelligence, etc
- structural changes – roles, reporting lines, team changes
- downsizing
- rapid growth
- culture change

The impact of not leading change effectively

When change is not carefully managed, people and teams can be dramatically affected. The introduction of the change is often perceived as sudden, even if the leader or the person creating the change has thought about it for a very long time. The reactions to the suddenness can make things fraught.

▌ It creates stress, which affects the mood. When this happens, conflict and unnecessary strain on relationships occur.

▌ Employees feel unsure and spend time speculating about the change, which takes focus away from their work. When this happens, energy and engagement levels drop, not to mention productivity. Time can be spent speculating the change rather than being productive.

▌ If a change is not properly thought through and planned, change implementation will be less effective and the employees will be less productive.

Change fatigue is another challenge for organisations. We live in a world of constant change. In fact, it is normal to live amongst rapid change. Change fatigue is something to be aware of. It can lead to people simply feeling overwhelmed with change and therefore becoming passive aggressive to the change. So they will nod, meaning, 'I heard you but I have no intention of doing anything because it will all change again very soon. I have seen all of this before.' They become passive in the change as they are tired of repetitive changes.

All these challenges have an impact on individuals and teams, leading to a drop in productivity, which is always costly.

Effective change benefits from both thoughtful, strategic change leadership as well as practical change management. They are constantly intertwined and we need both. A big part of change management is managing the change curve, which we will review in more detail in this chapter.

Let us reflect on and create a Roadmap for how to achieve change-driving impact. These steps include tools and tips to achieve your outcome.

The Change driving impact Roadmap

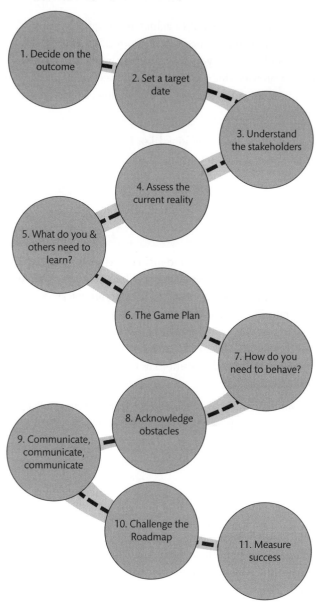

Roadmap step 1: decide on the outcome

So, what is it that you want to achieve? For what purpose do you want to drive change better, more effectively? Is there a specific change you are thinking about? The clearer you can be on this, the more pull it will have on you and the people involved, helping you make choices to move you towards it.

So, what could an outcome look like? Let us use an example. We will continue using this example throughout the chapter.

Anna's region is downsizing the main office and closing the others, being left with a small regional hub. As a rule, people will work remotely, using digital tools to communicate and collaborate. They are also moving to a new independent model of working, which involves great focus on output rather than input. This means each person can pretty much do their job the way they want to as long as they deliver the expected output.

Some employees like it, some do not. Some feel they will lose the social camaraderie, the ability to bounce ideas, which could impact creativity. Anna will need to lead differently, trusting people and giving them much greater freedom than before.

To make sense, any outcome should contribute to the overall vision and purpose of the organisation. There needs to be a red thread from the outcome you identify to each person's part in it. There has to be a compelling reason to drive change, rather than just 'it's the right thing to do'.

The outcome in this case can be described as: Anna wants her regional teams to fully have bought into the new work model and be ready to deploy it effectively from day 1.

Anna needs to find new leadership habits to successfully lead herself and her teams to make all this a reality.

This example shows how Anna is thinking through, as a leader, how to best impact her teams to see the value in the change, embrace it and become a part of it.

Fill in your change-driving outcome below – why you want people to embrace and help drive change better, faster or more effectively.

My change-driving outcome is:

Roadmap step 2: set a target date

By when do you want to achieve this? And, if there is not an obvious target date, do you need to create one? Deadlines focus the mind and start an internal clock ticking. Without a clear endpoint, things can drift and procrastination can kick in. What gets measured gets done.

In this chapter's story, there is a given deadline, where Anna knows the office closes or reduces in size in nine months' time.

What is your target date? Fill it in here.

> The target date is:

Roadmap step 3: understand the stakeholders

Who does this involve and impact? Who are your stakeholders? What do you know and understand about them? What more do you need to know about them?

There are mixed emotions about this change, and Anna is well aware of that. Some of her team members have asked for this flexible way of working for a long time. They are really onboard and could have a great positive, change-driving effect on their colleagues. Those who fear the change see it as a threat to teamwork and they question whether everyone will take responsibility when given all that freedom.

As digital solutions are at the heart of this setup, alignment with IT to make sure it all works as planned is crucial to avoid ending up in a blame scenario.

Anna has to deliver the changes and the cost reductions that they will bring to her boss, Stephen. He has been a part of a bigger change initiative and Anna has to deliver her regional targets along with her peers. Anna also wants to engage with her peers who lead other regions to ensure they are aligned on their approach. Customers need to be considered in the change and Anna wants to ensure the impact to them is minimal. In fact, they simply need to see that the change is for the better.

Anna wants to impact her team to create the change so her focus is on getting them to drive and own the changes needed, helping them to see the benefits and getting her team involved in influencing the other stakeholders too. If she does involve her team, then the change can be implemented more quickly.

> As Anna starts to analyse her stakeholders, she realises there are more people affected by this change and therefore connected to the change. Anna will have to work with her direct reports, her peers, her boss, the IT department and customers too. The awareness of this helps her to see the links between all of them and how she can lead this change. She also wants to 'put herself in the shoes of her team members' to think about the best way to get them to engage in this change, using those who are keen on the change to help to drive the change with those team members who are not so keen.

You must stop and reflect on the bigger picture, being strategic and consider each stakeholder individually as well as how they impact each other. Please complete your own stakeholder analysis below.

My stakeholders are:

This is what I know about them and their needs:

For more in-depth information on stakeholder planning, please go to Chapter 4.

Roadmap step 4: assess the current reality

Be realistic about where you currently are with regards to people's readiness level to embrace and help drive change for this specific outcome. Notice the difference between where you are right now and where you want to be (your outcome). How big is the gap? You really need to get a sense of how big or small the gap is so that you can make a realistic assessment of what it will take to close the gap. Do not be judgemental about it, accept the current reality as it is – it is not good, bad, right or wrong.

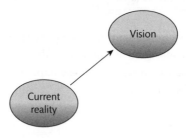

Whenever there is a gap between how things are now and how you want them to be, there is a natural tension that is created in that space. That tension can be described as an elastic band pulled taut between the current and future situation. Unless the desired outcome is strong enough to pull you out of the current reality, you will default back into current reality. So make sure the outcome you are after is very clear and shared with those whom it concerns.

> Anna was in the middle of a team meeting where her direct report team were discussing the downsizing and the new smaller regional hub. The main challenges the team were describing included the fear of not being together to share ideas and thoughts. They were also a team that liked to come together for social interaction, to make work fun and to bounce ideas around. They talked about the lack of teamwork and motivation they may experience in this new environment. How are we going to keep this up when we are based remotely and on our own?
>
> Anna observed some team members getting very vocal about all of this. The team were reminding themselves that, currently, they did not have the right tools to be able to work remotely effectively. In fact, they were even coming up with more reasons why this would be tough. Anna was afraid that the people on the team who were enthusiastic were becoming despondent.

Anna is experiencing frustration. She can see what needs to happen, she is closer to the change and has, indeed, been discussing it with Stephen for some time. She also acknowledges that she too had to go through her own frustrations with the downsizing before she could see the way forward. Now her team were doing the same thing. She wanted to rush them through so they could just get on with it. However, she recognised she needed to lead them through it. To do this, she had to acknowledge the change curve and where the team were in the change curve and where she was too.

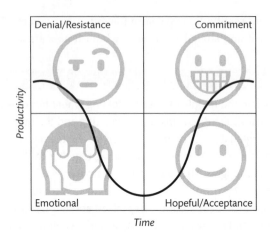

Phase 1 Denial/Resistance

When people are in the denial phase, you need to communicate, but do not give them too much at this point, not too much, too soon. Give them enough information, so that they understand that the change is happening, but do not overwhelm them. They need communication little and often. Make sure people know where to go for answers. Make sure you are available to answer questions to help them move through the change curve and into the next quadrant.

Phase 2 Emotional

During this phase, the fear, anger, resentment and uncertainty start to come into play. Team members may need to vent their anger and share how they feel. This is a normal human reaction that needs to happen. In carefully planning this phase, you need to have thought through the obstacles and objections people will bring up. Also, really think about the impact the change has. Be ready to listen and allow people to talk about what they are experiencing. If this is not led effectively, it can send you into chaos. People who do not feel like anyone understands what they are feeling tend to stay in the emotional phase. Be prepared to listen and help people to get answers to their concerns, so that they can move on to the next phase. You cannot force people through the change, otherwise you experience the passive aggressive reaction to change.

Phase 3 Hopeful/Acceptance

Employees are now moving towards the change; they are ready to explore more around what it means for them. They are also considering how they can start to make it work and can start to contribute with ideas for the change implementation. Be ready with any training, support or guidance here. This is where you can add value to their responses. Also, give them experiences of what the change will bring and what it will be like. Talk about and show them what it will be like when the change is implemented.

Phase 4 Commitment

The team have come through the change and accepted it and it is now happening. This is the point to celebrate success, to celebrate the achievements along the way. Remember how far you have come and appreciate that. This will reinforce the positives of the change and make it easier next time you want to implement change.

Anna was clearly in the commitment part of the change curve while her team were still in denial and resistance. As a leader, it is important to know this is happening, and then lead with that in mind. Anna was in denial and resistance when she first heard of the change but has now moved to the commitment phase over time herself. As a leader, this is part of leading change-driving impact. In fact, acknowledging the gap between where you are and others are on the change curve is probably the most important part of leading change.

> Anna's current reality is that there is fear of the change within the team, lots of speculation of how it will work and what it means for each person – the WIIFM (What's in it for me?). This is now affecting even those who were feeling OK about the change.

What does your current reality look like (in contrast to your outcome)? Write it down here.

> Our current reality looks like this:

What are you going to do with that distance, that natural tension that is created between the current reality and the desired outcome? Hold on to any ideas you are having – we will get to action planning in step 6.

Roadmap step 5: what do you and others need to learn?

What do you need to learn (about) to be able to do this?

What do your stakeholders need to learn?

With this change comes a need to learn, we all need to learn. Having a culture of always wanting to learn means we are more open to being creative and it forces us to look at things differently. This helps us to continue to be innovative.

Thinking we know everything is outdated; how can we in a world that changes so fast? Data suggests that 50 per cent of what is taught during the first year of a four-year technical degree is outdated by year three.[30] Even the most experienced of people have something they need to learn. In every situation, you need to challenge yourself and others in what needs to be learnt uniquely in each situation. Actually, having a step 5 in this Roadmap focuses you on reviewing what you need to learn, it gives you permission to not have to have all the answers. In a world of constant change, how can we possibly have all the answers? Even thinking you have all the answers is naive and outdated.

Anna's team were in different places with this change; it was taking time for them to get to understand what this change really meant. Lots of chatter was around' *Where will you work from' and 'how will I know where you are going to be? How will I know where everyone is and what we are all thinking about in terms of the issues we face or the tasks and actions we need to deliver? It feels like it could be chaotic. It feels like we almost need to reframe the way of working and get to some principles of how to work together in this new world.'* There was more time spent speculating than being productive.

The IT department had sent out some new ground rules for working, but the technology and the newness of them fuelled the chatter. Time to learn more about the support the team would be getting.

Anna has very little experience in leading remotely; she can do it, but she needs to pay attention to the different style she will need to adopt. Having to learn more about how to lead in a virtual world means she needs to pay more attention to *how* she is leading as well as *what* she is leading. Anna will need to trust people and people in the team will need to earn trust from her and with each other. They all have to learn about trust when they can no longer rely on being face to face in interactions.

Team members need to learn to work remotely. This will involve how to communicate. They will need to engage and learn the digital tools that will help them be successful. Anna will need to manage upwards to her boss Stephen, thinking carefully about how she keeps him updated and, therefore, increasing her own levels of trust with him.

What learnings are needed for you and your stakeholders? Capture your observations below.

This is what I need to learn about:

This is what my stakeholders need to learn about:

Roadmap step 6: the Game Plan

What needs doing?

Who will do it?

When will it be done?

Any effective change strategy and process starts by answering the question *why*. Why is the change happening and what will it lead to? Once you have identified that you need a strategy for change, just like you need strategies in other areas of the business, this Road Map with its Game Plan becomes your strategy. Start with why and keep coming back to that why constantly, make the links and connections to the bigger reason why.

There are a multitude of change leadership and management solutions. We focus here on some of the ones we have seen have the biggest impact on change buy-in. Reflect on these factors to identify the areas that would be relevant for you to focus on in your Game Plan.

1. **As a leader, how are you adding value?**

The more senior you are, the fewer answers you should have to have and the more questions you should be creating. This is one important way of adding value through change. The more you ask others questions, you get them to learn, grow and develop by finding the answers themselves. If leaders do this, then they are adding true value as a leader. You need to ask yourself 'How am I adding value as a leader/senior leader here?'

Some professions – news reporters, coaches, police investigators and lawyers – are trained to ask questions. Leaders, in particular, can benefit from becoming an expert at asking questions without it sounding like an interrogation. Skilful use of questions is an interaction, where the other party is invited in to engage in fluid conversation.

Some tips on effective questioning include the following:

▌ Be a good listener, if you don't ask you don't get, so make sure you ask questions.

▌ Asking more questions makes you a better questioner.

▌ When you are sitting listening to someone with your answer running, thinking 'this is what I want to say next' – stop yourself and think – 'What is the best question I could ask here to help this person get the answer'? This unlocks the other person's own learning and it improves the personal bond you have with them too.

▌ Use some follow up questions like:- 'what other suggestions do you have' and 'Explain more about. . . ' Know when to use open ended questions and when to use closed ones.

▌ Ask them with the right tonation. 'How did that happen'? can be said in so many ways with the emphasis on different words, it changes the meaning of the question.

> ▌ *How* did that happen?
>
> ▌ How *did* that happen?
>
> ▌ How did *that* happen?

2. The emotional aspect of change

Leaders need to carefully manage the change process with their team, to minimise the impact of distraction and worry, and to keep the team successful. Here are some things you can do when dealing with the emotional aspects of change:

▌ Discuss what is going on, and get fears and worries out into the open. One of the main reasons people resist or fear change is that they do not think/feel that anyone is aware of, or understands, their concerns. Once they know they are seen and heard, it becomes easier to move on – and to start finding constructive solutions. Make sure you have ongoing conversations with people – ask 'How are things going? How are you feeling? What can we do about it?'

▌ Focus people's attention onto possibilities and opportunities of the change; the challenges and the future.

▌ Avoid blame (it is never constructive and only drives defensive behaviour, which is detrimental to collaboration and teamwork).

▌ Quickly find practical solutions to get the team focused on tangible actions and behaviours that can drive results and show progress of the change.

3. **Use the positive change influencers**

What could go right? There is never just one way of looking at a situation. You probably know people who have expressed that some of the best things that have happened to them have come as a result of (unwanted) change.

Help your team to reframe a situation by exploring what it could bring from an optimistic standpoint. Ask team members to share the moments when they have experienced a good result during a time of uncertainty. Use a crisis to pull the team together. In addition to that, consider communicating what will not change. A 2018 study[31] shows that people embrace change more when they do not feel like the organisational identity is under threat, as they can see what is not changing.

4. **Do not waste time in the 'uncertainty void'**

Show that it is OK to make mistakes. Sometimes you win, sometimes you learn (from what went wrong). Use the disruption as a way for the team and its members to develop.

Remind the team of their purpose and how important their role is within the organisation. Stay focused on that purpose and get on with the task at hand. It is easy to slow down when faced with uncertainty. Keep the team moving forward. Adjust goals, plans and tasks, if needed, making sure the team keeps progressing.

5. **Slow down to speed up the change**

Leaders can sometimes operate at such a speed that they are too far ahead of the rest of the team. Stop and reflect to ensure you are prioritising the changes, doing the right thing at the right time.

6. **No one has all the answers**

In change it is more important than ever to work closely together. Encourage people to ask for help and for other's input. And ask for help yourself, as a leader – do not feel you have to have all the answers – no one can, it is as simple as that.

7. **Hold regular change meetings**

This may seem obvious, but you would be surprised how often this is overlooked. Have regular quick check-ins – face-to-face, on video call or phone. Make people feel that they are not alone, that you support each other. Have fun together and make time for laughter and casual conversations. Focus on the how, not just the what. Uncertainty and turbulence create questions. What will this mean for us? How will we resolve this? How will I be affected? Make sure you create frequent opportunities to talk as a team, so you understand concerns and hopes – and, where possible, provide answers.

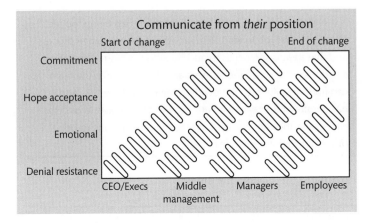

Communicate from their position

Anna knew from experience that team decisions would be helpful for her. Allowing the team to get involved and search for solutions together had always proved successful so she would do that again. Calling meetings to talk about this may feel like it is taking more time than necessary but, if she had not got people on board now, then she would have to go back and rework it all again, so this investment of time and energy was the right thing to do. She needed to get this into a plan as a draft to discuss with them. Saying it was a draft and not an 'absolute' was what she would do next. They could shape it together. Then she could involve Stephen and her peers.

Anna decides to get some change meetings into the agenda. In the next nine months these will have to be regular. She will do this as a mixture of virtual meetings via voice and video call, as well as some meetings in person. That way, she can get the team actually starting to experience the new way of working. Anna is going to build in some 'stop and reflect' time to force herself to ensure she is not moving faster than the team and is therefore bringing people with her rather than being too far ahead. It is her job to lead this team through the change process and that means she needs to add value to the team. She knows she does not have all the answers and that, together, the team can find the solutions on how they can make this work. Anna has people in the team who are positive change agents and she will ensure they are engaged in meetings and actions to bring others through the change curve.

Complete your Game Plan below.

What to do	How to do it	Who will do it	When will it get done	What impact will this have on collaboration?

Roadmap step 7: how do you need to behave?

How do you need to behave? How will those behaviours make others feel so that they want to engage with, buy into and help drive change more?

Here are a few factors to consider.

It starts with you. What are you role modelling?

The solutions you have identified in your Game Plan work best when carried out with supporting 'how to' behaviours.

The actions on their own will take you so far. With the right behaviours, you walk the talk and your change-driving impact is greater.

Behaviours are the differentiating factor in change. They are the magic key to whether the change happens or not. So many times, people focus on all the tasks and action plans but, if you want to make real change happen, then this is the differentiating factor.

Here are some change-driving behaviours to consider to create change leadership:

- Be proactive
- Be reflective
- Demonstrate responsibility
- Be positive
- Show empathy
- Be considerate
- Be trustworthy
- Be sensible
- Do not be afraid to be courageous
- Be open minded
- Demonstrate belief in the change
- Most importantly, stop and celebrate the success you have created

Anna is feeling excited by the changes, but is aware that her excitement is dwindling due to her team's not so positive reactions to the new way of working. Anna has to keep up her enthusiasm; she is a positive person and wants to use that

➤

strength. She wants to find optimism within herself, while being realistic, to allow her to help others to see the way through these changes. Her stress levels are showing and she does not like that; she does not want to show that to the team.

Anna is emotionally intelligent so is aware of how this is affecting and impacting her team. She is being more critical of them and is short and curt in her conversations, not giving much time to their concerns. Anna knows she has to take a look in the mirror and see what she is portraying to others. As a leader, she needs to demonstrate the right behaviours right now. Time to think about what she is role modelling and take control.

Many leaders think they can run ahead with the change and that people will just have to 'keep up' and 'get on with it'. Rarely does that strategy work. It does have an effect, but it takes longer. Even if leaders feel like they are moving fast, they are not. You have to take care of the human aspects of change and not underestimate its importance. The worst situation to have in times of change are those people who choose to opt out of the change but stay in the organisation. Opting out means they are there in body but not in soul. Leaders have a responsibility to deal with that for all stakeholders concerned as this can be a blocker to change.

Anna needs to continue to be positive, keep her enthusiasm and be realistic about the change, demonstrate she believes in the change, and not allow that negativity to stop her from what she believes is good change for the sake of the business. Anna has to talk about the bigger picture and, once again, state why this is happening, remembering all the great reasons for the change. Anna wants to remember where everyone is on the change curve; clearly they are not all in the same place as her.

So, how do you choose to behave to drive change?

This is how I choose to behave	This is how each of these behaviours will have an impact on the steps of my Game Plan

Roadmap step 8: acknowledge obstacles

What obstacles are there? Or could there be? How can they be overcome?

Common obstacles to effective change are:

- Not knowing the bigger picture 'why'
- Not understanding the WIIFM (what's in it for me?)
- Being stuck in the emotions and how the change feels
- Sticking with what we already know and so blocking the change
- No consequences for the change, not moving forward, not seeing the benefit of the change
- Not seeing how it all links together, nor the connections from the change to me
- People who opt out of the change but stay in the organisation spread the inertia
- Not really understanding the urgency for change

Anna had built such a strong team and was now concerned that they could not function in the new way. She had put so much emphasis on how they should work closely together. Now the new offices meant they could choose to work remotely as long as they produced the expected output. It was different for the team and Anna felt this camaraderie and teamwork was now an obstacle. Everyone had seen the benefits of sharing information and they had been pretty creative together, even winning an award as a team for it. Time was always an issue and, yet again, it felt like they just did not have time for this change.

Anna was going to have to use this strong team ethic to her advantage. While reviewing the obstacles, she decided to ask the team to think about what they had learned from working well together and recreate it with the new virtual world in mind. Anna was always busy and was sometimes given feedback to say she would rush through things just to 'get them done' to the detriment of relationships. She knew that this obstacle had to change as she was now more senior, so she wanted to pay attention to her reputation and impact. Ticking-the-box exercises like this were making her look more junior as a leader. A senior leader should have more strategic impact than that.

What obstacles do you see that need overcoming – for you, the team(s), the organisation?

```
┌─────────────────────────────────────────────────────┐
│  The obstacles I can foresee:                         │
│                                                       │
│                                                       │
│                                                       │
│                                                       │
│  How I will overcome them:                            │
│                                                       │
│                                                       │
│                                                       │
│                                                       │
│                                                       │
└─────────────────────────────────────────────────────┘
```

Roadmap step 9: communicate, communicate, communicate

What will you communicate? Who, when, how, to whom?
How do you need to be and behave in your communication?

Decide what to share and what not to share. Honesty is
one thing, sharing every single thought and fear would be
counterproductive.

Choose your response.

During change, people tend to focus on the stories and the
'grapevine', which can distract from getting the job done. Human
nature means people start to talk about what might happen
rather than the reality. Leaders need to work hard at keeping
people informed and communicating whatever they can. They
also need to engage people, give them whatever direction
they can and a future focus. This keeps people motivated and
productive through uncertain times. Communicate more not
less. People want to feel valued and to understand what is
happening while having as much communication as possible.
Getting people together and discussing what is happening and
how people feel is critical to ride the wave of change. Otherwise
people feel they are lost and do not know which way to go.

Follow these four principles of dealing with questions transparently:

1. Try to answer the question.

2. If you do not know an answer, say so.

3. If you cannot answer the question now, make a commitment for when you will and honour it.

4. If you know the answer but cannot say currently, say so and make a commitment to share information when you can.

Recognise that you are not at the same stage as others in relation to the change; sometimes as a leader you are one, two or three steps ahead of your team. Demonstrate empathy. Putting yourself into others' shoes forces you to acknowledge where they are.

When thinking about communication for a specific outcome, there are often two aspects of two-way communication that need particular attention.

The first one is *framing* – how will you frame the message overall, particularly when you first share it? Framing is very much about how you communicate, the words you use, the stories you tell, the way you help people see the importance in what you are saying. It is about communicating a message in such a way that you influence people to listen to you. How are you building in a feedback loop so you can get immediate input from those involved?

The second one is the structure and determination of ongoing progress and results communication needed to keep people motivated and help them see the progress made. This would, typically, involve frequency, method, channel and feedback loop.

In order to fill in the gaps in communication that otherwise people will fill in themselves, you have to communicate, communicate, communicate. Do not be fearful of stating the obvious. Just because it is obvious to you, it may not be obvious to others. Do not make the assumption that people already know. How can they? People always want the context.

Anna knows that she needs to build a communication map and clearly think about who she should communicate with at each point along the path. Anna chooses to be more strategic about her communication. She prepares a communication strategy for the change and a communication plan. It is becoming clear to her that it has to happen sooner rather than later. She has a lot of stakeholders involved now and taking it by chance is not an option.

Anna identifies the following key messages that her various stakeholders will benefit from hearing and being reminded of.

Her team:

▌ We are all in this together and we will create a plan together. You will have input and I will lead you through the changes.

▌ I will constantly explain and link to the bigger picture.

▌ I will support you and want to add value to this.

Her boss:

▌ Let me keep you informed. This is where I am, this is the progress we have made, this is what is next.

▌ This is where I need your support.

▌ My team needs your support.

▌ This is where I can support you.

IT department:

▌ This is how we will feed back our user experience to you.

▌ This is what you could do to support us in this change.

▌ This is how we can support you in this change.

What do you want your stakeholders to hear? Fill in the speech bubbles below.

Roadmap step 10: challenge the Roadmap

Challenge your draft Impact Roadmap – how could you think of all of this differently?

OK, let us question everything one more time. What if there was another way to achieve this change-driving outcome? Review what you have reflected on so far and ask yourself – how could I think of all this differently? Could there be a completely different approach to engage people in change and drive change effectively?

Leave it for a day and review again	Ask a friend!
Talk to a peer	Talk to your team

Look at it from a new perspective by imagining yourself as someone else–a few examples below (imagine how they would look and sound)–what would they do?
Your prime minister or president?
Your parents?
Nelson Mandela?
Your university leader or teacher?
Or someone else!

Or are there any additional ideas that you want to add to your plan so far?

When challenging my current thinking, this is what I come up
with:

Roadmap step 11: measure the success

How are you going to measure your change-driving outcome?
How will you know if you have achieved the kind of change
buy-in and progress you were aiming for? How will you ensure
you follow through and follow up on your way to achieving
the outcome? And how will you celebrate the success?

Anna is having a review with the team every two weeks. At
this review session, they will specifically talk about what is
going well, asking each team member, 'What do we need to
celebrate personally and as a team?' This will ensure people
are celebrating as they go along rather than just at the end
when the change is implemented.

Anna knows that the team will deliver on the change. Together,
they will agree, 'how we will know when we have been
successful'. A team meeting together in person, which will be a
rare occurrence, will be the reward in itself!

To celebrate successes is always important, but particularly
so when facing turbulence. That is when the pat on the
back and sense of achievement can really make a difference.

Celebrate the milestones and encourage continued effort. Be proud of your team – and show it.

How will you make sure you follow through and measure and celebrate success?

This is how I will follow through and follow up:

This is how I will measure success:

This is how I will celebrate success:

THE EFFECT ON CULTURE

Transformational, lasting change happens at a behavioural level. Change and handling change is happening in every organisation around the world, no matter how big or small. You already have a culture, a way of dealing with change. Whether you pay attention to it or not, it is there.

If you want to create a culture of change, then you have to work out *how* you handle change as a leader, how that ripples to your team and peers and, through them, the rest of the organisation. Change is a reality in all workplaces, but it is not always done well. When you are able to help people embrace the change and engage with it, it becomes a natural part of how the organisation operates through successful change.

Now that you have worked your way through how you will lead to achieve change-driving impact, you may also want to transfer your notes and create a complete plan by filling in the Impact Roadmap Worksheet at the back of the book or by downloading it from www.2020visionleader.com/ ImpactRoadmap.

Self-assessment

Now that you have created your Impact Roadmap, please review
the progress you have made by completing this self-assessment.

How would you rate your ability to create change-driving impact in
these areas?

	1 Very poor	2 Poor	3 Just OK	4 Good	5 Excellent
Helping people to embrace change					
Getting people to help drive change					
Allowing people to work together to create change					

Intelligence is the ability to adapt to change.

Stephen Hawking

10

Innovative impact

> **LEADERSHIP FACT**
>
> **Did you know?**
>
> Employees who receive strong recognition are 33 per cent more likely to be proactively innovating and generate twice as many ideas per month compared to those who are not recognised well.[32]

Self-assessment

Before reading this chapter, do the following quick self-assessment.

How would you rate your ability to create innovative impact in these areas?

	1 Very poor	2 Poor	3 Just OK	4 Good	5 Excellent
Releasing people's innovative potential					
Driving continuous innovation					
Getting people excited about innovative challenges					

The case for innovation

Innovate or die!

You have probably heard this said by people like Jack V. Matson and Peter Drucker and many others over the years.

And they are right. The future holds challenges that we know nothing about. The increasing speed of change in the world of business, and in society as a whole, makes us realise that we need to become more and more innovative to find the solutions that are needed for the future.

Yes, innovation is key and you can help make it happen. You can have innovative impact.

Leaders set the tone in an organisation for what is expected, what is acceptable and what is the norm. Leaders can do a lot to create an environment where the kind of innovation the future demands can flourish.

Many organisations have 'innovation' as a buzzword in their values or vision and mission statement, but what is the differentiating factor between the ones that really innovate and those that do not? The behaviours that support the intentions and actions matter greatly here.

This chapter gives an opportunity to think about and plan for how you can make innovation into a habit for yourself, your team, your organisation. How can you make it desirable and fun to continuously not just challenge the status quo but also to create something completely new and different? How can you release that innovative potential in others for the organisation to be able to stay relevant or even stay ahead of the trends?

Disrupt or be disrupted!

This is increasingly becoming the norm, and you can be that positive disruptor who unleashes that kind of thinking and being. You can help shape a curious, boundary-pushing, innovative culture. And impact, as discussed earlier, is largely down to the way you role model behaviours that engage people, in this case to innovate.

Be a 'disruptive leader'!

People often perceive disruption as something negative, and it certainly can be. Someone's behaviours can be disruptive and unhelpful in a meeting, for example. But that is not what we are talking about here. No, we have experienced when being disruptive can be very positive.

To disrupt is to do something that radically changes the status quo and, at the speed of change that we are experiencing in society today, organisations will either disrupt *or* be disrupted by old or new players on the market. This is the kind of leadership the future needs: leaders who can navigate, lead and collaborate through the choppy waters of constant change.

A 2018 study[33] by McKinsey describes the big paradigm shift that is going on in organisations now, where the old paradigm of organisations as machines is being challenged by trends such as continuously changing environment and disruptive technology.

The new paradigm, the new reality, is one of the organisation as a living organism, that needs to adapt and change and respond to the fast-paced change – a nimble, agile entity. This is a big challenge, for many large organisations in particular, to adapt to this new reality and become nimble and responsive in the way that is needed.

It is challenging, yes, but doable. This is where the concept of leaders as disruptors comes in.

Working with organisations around the world, supporting them in navigating a constantly changing world and reflecting on the latest research on future leadership, we have identified five steps that leaders can take to be positive disruptors in the digital age.

The five agile steps for disruptive leaders

1. Build your strategic ability

Are you strategic? Are you strategic enough?

Many leaders we meet, unless quite senior, are focused on the tactical, day-to-day realities of work. That is OK, but there needs to be a balance, for everyone, regardless of our role – everyone needs to weave in strategy in what they do. And, in order to be a positive disruptor, it is absolutely crucial to focus on and develop strategic ability. That strategic ability can be broken down into a number of skills, which can be developed.

We have found these five strategic thinking skills to be crucial in building strategic ability:

Systems thinking

Be curious about the world around you to understand the system you are in – observe, listen and explore it. When it comes to systems thinking, usually, there are two main systems to consider – the internal system of the organisation and the external system, which is everything outside the organisation that touches it in some way: market, competitors, social, political and financial environment, etc. The more you know about your systems, the more likely you are to spot or create relevant opportunities for innovation, as well as understand the impact the organisation has and can have.

Purpose and vision focus

Begin with the end in mind. Be relentlessly purpose-driven, and become super-focused on the organisational vision and reason for being. This kind of passion can have a big impact on others, igniting their passion for the vision and purpose too. Show that everything is done for a reason – keep explaining and linking actions: why they are being done and what they will lead to. Doing something for a reason is engaging; it is an opportunity for everyone to know that they truly make a difference.

Long-term thinking

Plan for the future, set long-term goals (alongside your short-term goals). Focus on the relationships that are crucial for long-term success. This could be clients, suppliers, potential clients and colleagues – just to mention a few. By being respectful and collaborative now you can create a respectful and collaborative relationship over time, which is not just the right thing to do, but it will also make it easier to get them to want to work with you in the future.

Taking responsibility for the whole

Remind yourself of the big picture, take a step back to see beyond your own responsibility today. Recognise that success requires shared responsibility. Look for linkages and interactions between tasks and people, e.g. who is dependent on whom, where are the handoffs, etc. Think through the effects of decisions and actions, projecting that into the future. Keep in mind, though, that this is hard to do alone, so find others you can work with to figure this out. Assess the impact of strategies, plans, actions and behaviours, to avoid acting in a here-and-now way.

Asking strategic questions

Provide strategic focus to dialogues. Influence others to take a strategic view and build their strategic ability by asking strategic questions, such as: *Where do we want to be? For what purpose are we doing what we are doing? How will this differentiate us from others (competitors)? Where are we now? How will we get there? What will be the impact of those actions, now and later?*

2. Leave your ego at the door

We all have egos and, at times, they positively spur us on, they keep us focused and going. But egos can also be detrimental to success. Egos can make us blind to new thoughts and ideas for innovation, if we are fearful of 'losing face' or appearing as if we do not have all the answers. Egos can make us hold on to 'old truths', hence being reluctant to listen to and open up to other people or try new things.

This is what we mean, in more detail, by *leaving your ego at the door,* and how it can be achieved:

Share leadership

Gone are the days when leaders ruled from their office on the top floor. The leadership of the future is much more inclusive and shared. Effective, disruptive leaders recognise that they need others to share leadership with them, for different people to step forward at different times to advise, to guide and/or to lead, based on knowledge, skills, experience and other unique and valuable contributions.

Be authentic and transparent

No one is perfect and that is exactly how it should be. Dare to be an authentic leader who is transparent about your learning journey and recognise that true progress requires non-perfect results, which creates innovation and better results. Leaders who dare put their guard down and share that they, at times, struggle (and *learn*) like everyone else will be able to connect more effectively with others. Authentic stories create emotional connections, rather than just intellectual. Find your unique stories that can create insight, hope and inspiration for others. Dare to take off 'your corporate cloak' and let people get to know the authentic person, not just a polished façade.

Be bold in your collaborations

The challenges and opportunities of the future are best dealt with through collaboration, where different players come together to give their unique, relevant input. Dialogue sparks more dialogue, ideas feed ideas and creative cross-pollination of ideas and insight can drive innovative solutions. To be a positive disruptor is to realise that new, innovative, collaborative connections can always be created. Challenge your thinking and consider new collaborative partners for given challenges and opportunities. Why not collaborate with your most vocal and critical stakeholders, local government or even competitors? Think about it, who could you collaborate with to find those new answers to new challenges?

Dare to seize opportunities

Once you understand the 'system' you are in, it is easier
to spot the opportunities around you that are relevant and
can be acted upon. We are surrounded by opportunities
and seizing such an opportunity, without being guaranteed
a specific outcome, can sometimes be daunting. And yet, if
we do not, we certainly will not reap any rewards. Think
about how you can be a measured, sensible risk-taker, who
does not let the fear of a slightly bruised ego stop you from
making the most of relevant and viable opportunities. It
is never a question of going for everything – it is about
having the confidence to give it a go.

Dare to speak up

Maybe you have got a great answer or maybe you have a
great opportunity for learning. Organisations, and society
overall, need straight-talking people who speak their
mind, who are not just keeping quiet when they have
ideas, suggestions and different opinions. Speaking up
takes drive, interest and passion – and innovation thrives
on it. Find those in yourself and become a respectful,
collaborative voice of progress for the future.

Try, learn and adjust

Build the courage to try things out, instead of just holding
on to tried and tested approaches. Dare to try. By trying
and testing something new, then evaluating it, learning can
happen, which in turn triggers adjustment and forward
movement. Think about it, how could you create an
environment where this type of fast learning takes place?
Who do you need to collaborate with to make it happen?
Maybe you are facing a challenge right now where you
could bring together *all* the five aspects listed above?

3. Take teaming and collaboration to a new level

To come together as a team and to collaborate is
something we humans have done – in fact, our survival
has depended on it – from the beginning of time.

In a globalised world of fast-paced change, we need each other now more than ever. At work, that means teaming and collaboration increasingly needs to be seen and used as a major driver of innovation, continuous business transformation and sustainable, long-term results.

As a positive disruptor, you must focus on this important driver. We talked extensively about collaborative impact in Chapter 8, but here are a few additional ways of doing just that:

- Promote a new way of thinking about teams. Prepare people for role mobility. Agility involves being able to come together as a team quickly as and when needed – and being able to take action.

- Empower your team(s) to be able to make decisions and take action.

- Embrace and demand diversity and learning in your team(s) – enable diverse input and new thinking (instead of risking an echo chamber).

4. Give enough stability so people can act with agility

In a constantly changing world, people often hesitate and become unsure about how to proceed, what to do and what is expected. This is perfectly normal, but it can impact progress and, hence, the more you can provide enough stability and certainty so that people feel confident to move into action and do what needs doing, the better.

Here are three key things to think about to make that a reality:

Make change a natural and desired part of life

Move from change management to change leadership – be more proactive about making the relevant change happen rather than just responding to changes that happen.

Talk to your team about how important constant change is – in order to survive and thrive in a world that keeps changing at great speed, whether we want it to or not. Make it super clear that constant change is the new status quo and we may as well fully embrace it and make it work for us.

Include your team in dialogue about the possible benefits of change, and find the answers and the tangible steps to success together.

Reward and recognise people for how they embrace change and dare to try, learn and progress.

Create structure and processes that enable empowered teams and agility

If your team is going to be able to manoeuvre a constantly changing playing field, they will be greatly helped by clarity of *how* to do that. Now, that is not to say that they will have all the specific answers. They do, however, need clear work processes that show how to explore reality, analyse data and make decisions and then act, without having to wait for much guidance or approval.

It needs to be clear and easy to do one's job, even as things are changing. Those leaders and organisations that are able to do that will increase their chances for success. Remember to weave evaluation and learning into your processes too – so that you can quickly learn from the results achieved and adapt, innovate and navigate successfully for the next steps.

Use the technology – make it easy and straightforward to communicate and collaborate

Review the digital solutions available to you and your team. Do you have what you need? And do you use it in the best way possible?

There are so many digital tools out there: email, collaboration platforms, intranets and many more.

Sometimes, a big range of options is inefficient, if people use different tools and end up wasting time trying to find a message from someone. Do not get lost in the plethora of tools available. Make a strategic decision about how to use your digital tools – what tool for what purpose? Where do you share documents? Where do you discuss subjects? Where do you share best practices, etc? Carefully choose and agree which one to use for what. This saves a lot of time and frustration and can quickly enhance collaboration too.

The more you can provide the kind of clarity, structure and stability that makes it easy for people to spot opportunities, be able to move quickly and nimbly, the better set up for the future you and your team/organisation will be.

5. Think H2H – human to human

In an increasingly digital world, our need for human interaction is probably more important than ever. That is where it happens, the connection, the passion, the innovation and disruption – together, between people, tapping into the most human aspect of us, our emotions. Having a 'human to human' focus is all about behaviours and the impact those have on others. So, remember to stay close to people. Care about the people around you, not just as co-worker, but as a human being. See them, hear them, value them, make them feel important. Help them see how they make a difference.

Find inspiration in yourself to inspire others and engage others through your own authentic engagement. Simply put – focus on the human aspect, being a human being, not just a 'human doing'.

Let us reflect on and create a Roadmap for how to achieve innovative impact. These steps include tools and tips to achieve your outcome.

The Innovative impact Roadmap

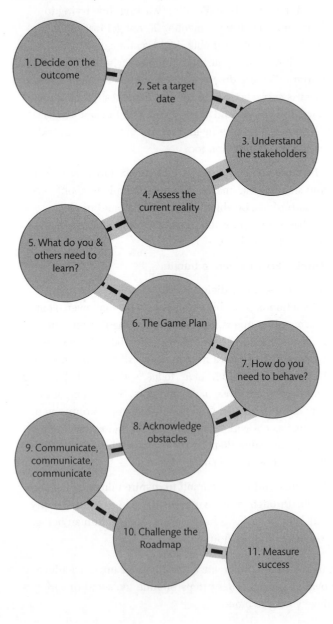

Roadmap step 1: decide on the outcome

So, what is it that you want to achieve? For what purpose do you want to innovate better, more effectively? Is there a specific innovative challenge that you are facing? The clearer you can be on this, the more pull it will have on you and the people involved, helping you make choices to move you towards it.

So, what could an outcome look like? Let us use an example. We will continue using this example throughout the chapter.

A number of new innovative insurance providers are appearing on the marketplace. Known for her creative thinking, Sophia has been asked to join a new global strategic innovation hub. The task of this hub is to do some blue sky thinking about how they can provide the kind of interaction, products and services that customers may not even know they were looking for yet! They need to 'innovate or die'. Sophia shares responsibility for engaging employees across the world to get involved in the needed innovation dialogue and, together, the innovation hub needs to get this going in six months. They need the creative power of as many people as possible to feed their thoughts and observations (from their unique work- and customer-related perspective). The company, ultimately, wants to create a more innovative culture.

To make sense, any outcome should contribute to the overall vision and purpose of the organisation. There needs to be a red thread from the outcome you identify to each person's part in it. There has to be a compelling reason to innovate, rather than just 'it's the right thing to do'.

> The outcome in this case can be described as kick-starting a new way of working internally with innovation, engaging people in an ongoing innovation dialogue. Longer term, they are also looking for innovative solutions to be created, but the first milestone is to lay the groundwork for the creation of an innovative culture.

Fill in your innovative outcome below – why you want to release people's innovative potential in order to drive innovation.

> My innovative outcome is:

Roadmap step 2: set a target date

By when do you want to achieve this? And, if there is not an obvious target date, do you need to create one? Deadlines focus the mind and start an internal clock ticking. Without a clear endpoint, things can drift and procrastination can kick in. What gets measured gets done.

> In this chapter's story, the innovation hub's remit is to have embedded a new way of engaging employees in innovative dialogue within six months.

What is your target date? Fill it in here.

The target date is:

Roadmap step 3: understand the stakeholders

Who does this involve and impact? Who are your stakeholders? What do you know and understand about them? What more do you need to know about them?

Sophia reflects on the key people involved and recognises that their stakeholders are employees overall, but also the executive leadership team and all other layers of leadership. Employees have so far not been expected to have much innovative input, and it has only really happened on an ad-hoc basis, in a random way. For this reason, their readiness level for getting involved may be low. And, yet, employees' buy-in to the idea of shared responsibility around innovation is crucial. Senior leaders are the sponsors of this initiative and express support of it. Operative leaders, apart from being expected to get engaged in the dialogue themselves at times, need to support employees in doing so – making it easy for them to be involved.

Innovation involves everyone and the desire from the organisation's point of view is to create a new culture of innovation, so Sophia recognises that her stakeholders include all employees, including its leaders on all levels. She needs to think carefully about how to approach the three main groups she has identified: employees, leaders and senior leaders (sponsors).

> As Sophia's stakeholders are both employees and leaders, she decides that she needs to find out how innovation (when it has happened) has worked so far and what has made people want to get involved. *What is it that has made people want to get involved?*
>
> Sophia needs to ensure they really have the support of the senior leaders, as expressing support is not necessarily a guarantee for support in reality.
>
> Operative leaders, she realises, may have concerns about how time-consuming this initiative will be and therefore Sophia needs to talk to them, sound them out and understand their concerns so they can be addressed.

You must stop and reflect on the bigger picture, be strategic and consider each stakeholder individually as well as how they impact each other.

Please complete your own stakeholder analysis below.

> My stakeholders are:
>
>
>
>
> This is what I know about them and their needs:

For more in-depth information on stakeholder planning, please go to Chapter 4.

Roadmap step 4: assess the current reality

Be realistic about where you currently are with regard to releasing people's innovative potential for this specific outcome. Notice the difference between where you are right now and where you want to be (your outcome). How big is the gap? You really need to get a sense of how big or small the gap is so that you can make a realistic assessment of what it will take to close the gap. Do not be judgemental about it, accept the current reality as it is – it is not good, bad, right or wrong.

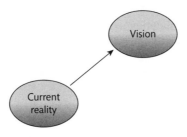

Whenever there is a gap between how things are now and how you want them to be, there is a natural tension that is created in that space. That tension can be described as an elastic band pulled taut between the current and future situation. Unless the desired outcome is strong enough to pull you out of the current reality, you will default back into current reality. So, make sure the outcome you are after is very clear and shared with those whom it concerns.

> Innovation is not something that has been on everyone's agenda before, so Sophia assesses that they are far from the desired outcome. It is not that people do not want to innovate but they have not been specifically asked to do it before and there may, therefore, be a lack of confidence for doing so. There is also not a process in place yet for how the innovative dialogue will work. There may also be structural issues that make this difficult – lack of effective dialogue tools, for example. The gap between current reality and vision/outcome is big. Innovation is not a part of the current culture, for sure.

Sophia is not surprised about the big gap, but she realises that they are facing quite a challenge to close that first gap in as little as six months. It will take real dedication and careful planning and coordination to achieve the stated outcome. She will need to stay calm and focused.

Sophia describes the current reality as: there is no innovative process, or dialogue tools, in place, employees have low individual experience/readiness level and potentially low confidence for it. We do not have a culture of innovating.

What does your current reality look like (in contrast to your outcome)? Write it down here.

Our current reality looks like this:

What are you going to do with that distance, that natural tension that is created between the current reality and the desired outcome? Hold on to any ideas you are having – we will get to action planning in step 6.

Roadmap step 5: what do you and others need to learn?

What do you need to learn (about) to be able to do this?

What do your stakeholders need to learn?

Impact, as well as innovation, are skills that can be learnt. If wanting to have greater innovative impact, consider what you could learn about the innovative process that would develop your own skills as well as being able to convey the need for innovation to others.

Sophia and her colleagues have reflected on the reality that innovation is not an organisational habit in their company. Sophia, therefore, reasonably assumes that the understanding of the innovative process and the skills involved are low. She also knows that, although she herself likes creative thinking, it is more of a natural ability rather than a polished skill. For that reason, she recognises she also needs to learn more about the subject. Sophia has never taken on a task before where she needs to have a conscious impact on so many people, which in itself is a challenge she wants to overcome.

> Sophia decides to learn more about innovation overall:
> innovation skills, tools, models and processes. On top of that,
> she must review how to best work with such a large stakeholder
> group, to communicate in a most effective and impactful way.
>
> She will then find or design an innovation learning intervention
> where creative thinking and innovation learning can happen
> and be applied for the stakeholders.

What learnings are needed for you and your stakeholders?
Capture your observations below.

This is what I need to learn about:

This is what my stakeholders need to learn about:

Roadmap step 6: the Game Plan

What needs doing?

Who will do it?

When will it be done?

Gone are the days when people could hold on to information,
thinking that 'knowledge is power'. The speed of change
means that unhelpful competitive thinking is no longer
desirable or sensible. The era of openness and even more
transparency is upon us.

Any organisation that wants to raise levels of innovation and change progression needs to proactively get their employees communicating better, generously sharing what they know, their expertise, insights and experience, as well as their ideas.

Let us look at some ways you can release people's innovative potential and make innovation a habit going forward.

Build innovation confidence

'I'm not creative.' We often hear people say that, and yet we know that is not true. Everyone has the ability to be creative, to contribute to an innovative dialogue and thereby drive innovation. Help people believe in their ability to be creative, encourage and push people to try it out and give their valuable input. Praise people when they get involved and tell them how it made a difference, how they had an impact on the outcome – make the links, make it easy to see so that getting involved feels normal or even a given.

Run PODS™ (power of dynamic sharing)

Use the brain powerhouse that is your organisation! At regular intervals, invite people to come together for the purpose of sharing all they know on a given subject. Increasingly, the speed of change means people do not have all the information they need. In fact, it is impossible to have all the information. Make the group as diverse as possible to get a wide range of views. And make sure you have a clear expected outcome. *Why are we sharing this?* People must understand there is a relevant and important purpose. Someone needs to facilitate to make sure there is fair sharing and everyone gets heard. Be prepared for – and invite – conflicting views, then manage the process carefully and ensure that key points are drawn out and captured. There must be a conclusion on how to use the shared information in the future, so the next step is to communicate the outcome and next steps.

Run internal and/or external 'hackathons'

Take inspiration from the world of hackathons, where programmers come together during a short period of time, intensively working together to 'hack away' at old ways of doing something. Bring employees (and maybe even customers) together for a day or two to create a new product or service. The time constraint involved in hackathons is a great driver for focusing the mind and making it happen.

Use conflict to drive innovation

Do not fear conflict, welcome it for its innovative powers and use it carefully and respectfully. Talk about how different ideas and opinions lead to something better to encourage the team members to openly and honestly share their thoughts. If your team is hesitant to share their knowledge, intuitions and opinions, then temporarily you may have a quiet, seemingly calm team situation, but, sooner or later, it will result in greater divides between people, emotional outbursts and even team members who decide to leave the team. Managing team conflict is everyone's responsibility, but leaders clearly need to take the lead to foster a climate of open exchange by encouraging people to talk, share, discuss and make decisions as a team. If a leader does this, then he/she can create a very powerful team where the efforts of a team can be multiplied along with the results because team members who have experienced conflict and resolved it grow stronger together.

Go and find the problems or opportunities – and start innovating

Encourage employees to actively look for problems; processes that are not working, unnecessary practices, handover breakdowns – as well as opportunities yet untapped: new industry practices, new target groups, customer interests. When everyone starts to come together and look for opportunities for innovation, step by step it builds a new habit of innovation.

Sophia is eager to put a detailed, specific Game Plan together. She knows that it will help her get the focus right, homing in on the activities that will make the biggest difference. She intends to create a step-by-step plan, outlining what to do each week and month, linked to the various stakeholder groups. Sophia is well aware that this is not something she should do on her own, though. She will need input not just from her Innovation Hub peers but also from a few key stakeholders – employees, leaders and senior leaders. Getting their input will increase her chances of buy-in to the whole initiative.

Very few people enjoy being told what to do. In fact, as Daniel H. Pink so eloquently points out in the book *Drive*, autonomy is one of the key drivers of intrinsic motivation. When we are given the chance to have a say over how we do things, we are more likely to actually do it. Why wouldn't we? We have created it!

Sophia decides to create an innovation learning intervention, as well as creating the structured innovation process, i.e. how, when and where people will be invited to become involved. She will include PODS™ and hackathons in that process. On top of that, with the support of leaders, she will work on building innovation confidence in the organisation.

Complete your Game Plan below.

What to do	How to do it	Who will do it	When it will get done	What impact will this have on innovation?

Roadmap step 7: how do you need to behave?

How do you need to behave? How will those behaviours make others feel so that they want to engage in and contribute to the organisation's innovative efforts?

Here are a few factors to consider.

It starts with you. What are you role modelling? How much are you getting involved in the innovative dialogue?

The solutions you have identified in your Game Plan work best when carried out with supporting 'how to' behaviours. The actions on their own will take you so far. With the right behaviours, you walk the talk and your innovative impact is greater.

Let us get practical. Here are six leadership behaviours that can help create an innovative culture and environment.

Be curious

Let go of any 'need to be right', get rid of any sense of prestige and openly admit that you do not know everything,

no one does. Listen without prejudice. Show that you value
people's differences and different opinions. Great innovation
leaders are curious and open-minded, realising that what
they knew yesterday may already be outdated. Great leaders
do not get complacent, they keep looking outwards and
inwards to see what is going on: what is happening in the
world, what society needs, what customers need, what
opportunities exist, what problems need solving, how to
thrive in the long-term.

Be inclusive and generous

No one has all the answers. By sharing your leadership with
others, by including others in discussions and decisions,
a multitude of ideas and inspiration can start to cross-
pollinate, enabling the creation of new ideas and solutions
for innovative results. Great innovative leaders continuously
invite their employees and other stakeholders to open,
explorative dialogue that challenges the status quo.

Be relentlessly customer-centric

Have customers and their needs at the front of your mind at
all times. Keep looking at things from their point of view:
what do they need, what do they want, how can you make
their lives easier? Consider the impact on customers in all
you do. Be genuinely interested, walk the talk.

Think long term

Business is so much more than the 'here and now', yet it is
easy to get caught up in the urgencies of the moment. And,
as much as this is needed, forward-looking leaders are able
to balance long- and short-term thinking, by setting goals and
creating plans to achieve that balance. They spend a good
chunk of time in the strategic, future space. Great innovation

leaders continuously invest in R&D, budgeting with a long-term focus – investing for the future and sustainable business results.

Be courageous and resilient

With changes and progress come mistakes. There is no way that everything that is tried becomes a success. Indeed, some of the greatest innovations and results come from daring to try and learning from mistakes. Just look at Thomas Edison's famous 'mistake' where he tried thousands of times to invent the lightbulb! Imagine if he had given up! But he did not. He had the courage to keep trying new things and the resilience to not give up despite the setbacks. 'Innovation impact' leaders encourage and coach others to take calculated risks and to learn from them. They are OK to shut ideas down if they do not work, not seeing it as failure but merely as new results to get closer to what is new and different. 'There is no such thing as failure, only results' is how they think.

Coach for innovation

Everyone can benefit from regular coaching, especially in a fast-changing world. Notice what your employees do and help them to hold up a metaphorical mirror on the work they do and how they perform it. This helps employees to keep learning and developing in line with the need for innovation and progress. Coaching leaders give people really good, specific feedback and observations on what went well and what could have gone better, all with the positive intent of creating learning. They create a learning culture by helping others to succeed and this allows for innovation to take place.

> Transformational, lasting change happens at a behavioural level.

Transformational, lasting change happens at a behavioural level, so these six behaviours are a good place to start to achieve innovative impact and success. Leaders have to create a learning culture in themselves, as leaders and in others to make innovation *really* happen.

Sophia is becoming increasingly aware of her own learning gap when it comes to innovation, and she does not want this to come across as a shortcoming. She understands she must take control of how she behaves and comes across to her stakeholders to ensure their support and buy-in. Sophia is determined to boost her own confidence in her abilities first so she can naturally and authentically display her commitment to innovation – and her own learning plan will help with that. She knows she needs to be a consistent role model for innovation through her behaviours.

Sophia chooses to focus particularly on the following behaviours as she engages with stakeholders around the organisation: being curious and listening well, being courageous in speaking up, sharing ideas and trying new things (admitting that she does not have all the answers), being optimistic and always looking for possible solutions.

So, how do you choose to behave to release and drive innovation? The six behaviours above is not a complete list. Refer back to impactful behaviours in other chapters if you want more ideas.

This is how I choose to behave	This is how each of these behaviours will have an impact on the steps of my Game Plan

Roadmap step 8: acknowledge obstacles

What obstacles are there? Or could there be? How can they be overcome?

According to a 2018 survey for innovation leaders, these are the top five obstacles to innovation in large companies.[34] The percentages show how many of the 270 leaders indicated these as obstacles.

- Politics, turf war, lack of alignment (55 per cent)
- Cultural issues (45 per cent)
- Inability to act on critical signals or development (42 per cent)
- Lack of budget (41 per cent)
- Lack of strategy or vision (36 per cent)

These findings are further complemented by a study by BlessingWhite,[35] which outlines the following barriers to internal innovation.

1. No longer having the intent to innovate
2. Employees not understanding what kinds of innovations are needed

3. Not considering enough options (locking in on one option too early)

4. Innovative ideas are perceived to be inconsistent with current business models

5. Established organisations often asking employees to prove an idea will work before giving permission to take action

6. Silo working stops the needed cross-silo teams to progress innovation

7. Work environment challenges: getting access to talent, structures, cultural norms and leadership support

The organisation tends to work in functional silos where employees interact and communicate with each other only when there is a burning reason to. This means there is very little creative exchange across functions and, to some degree, even within functions due to time constraints.

So far, there has not been much communication about the competitive challenges the company is facing. This means the awareness of what kind of innovation is needed is just not there.

The Innovation Hub recognises that silo working is a major obstacle as is employees not knowing what innovation is needed. This is why they will work closely with the executive team in rethinking the current silo habits and how the silos can be broken down as well as further clarifying and then communicating the specific innovation needs.

What obstacles do you see that need overcoming – for you, the team(s), the organisation?

The obstacles I can foresee:

How I will overcome them:

Roadmap step 9: communicate, communicate, communicate

What will you communicate? Who, when, how, to whom?
How do you need to be and behave in your communication?

When thinking about communication for a specific outcome, there are often two aspects of two-way communication that need particular attention.

The first one is *framing* – how will you frame the message overall, particularly when you first share it? Framing is very much about how you communicate, the words you use, the stories you tell, the way you help people see the importance in what you are saying. It is about communicating a message in such a way that you influence people to listen to you. How are you building in a feedback loop so you can get immediate input from those involved?

The second one is the structure and determination of ongoing progress and results communication needed to keep people motivated and help them see the progress made. This would, typically, involve frequency, method, channel and feedback loop.

As this will be a new way of working together across the organisation, it will be important to communicate at regular intervals with all the stakeholders to build their interest in and support for the initiative. They all need to be able to see that it is worthwhile doing, that it will lead to tangible results.

Sophia identifies the following key messages that her various stakeholders will benefit from hearing and being reminded of.

Employees:

▌ You play a crucial role in the company's future.

▌ We need your brain powerhouse, we need your professional insights and your creative thinking!

▌ This is why innovation is so important for us all.

Senior leaders/sponsors:

▌ You are role models for the kind of innovation we need, to break new ground in the industry.

▌ You can break down the barriers to innovation created by our current structure.

▌ This is the progress we have made.

Other leaders:

▌ You can help your employees engage in innovation by . . .

▌ This is how we can support you . . .

▌ These are the results we are expecting to achieve . . .

▌ This is why innovation is so important for us.

What do you want your stakeholders to hear? Fill in the speech bubbles below.

Roadmap step 10: challenge the Roadmap

Challenge your draft impact Roadmap – how could you think of all of this differently?

OK, let us question everything one more time. What if there was another way to achieve this innovation outcome? Review what you have reflected on so far and ask yourself – how could I think of all this differently? Could there be a completely different approach to releasing people's innovative potential and drive innovation more dynamically/effectively?

This process of completing this exercise in itself means you have to be innovative!

Leave it for a day and review again	Ask a friend!
Talk to a peer	Talk to your team

Look at it from a new perspective by imagining yourself as someone else–a few examples below (imagine how they would look and sound)–what would they do?
Usain Bolt
Your neighbour
Coco Chanel
Your elected politician
Or someone else!

Or are there any additional ideas that you want to add to your plan so far?

> When challenging my current thinking, this is what I come up with:

Roadmap step 11: measure the success

How are you going to measure your innovation outcome? How will you know if you have achieved the level of innovative engagement and output you were aiming for? How will you ensure you follow through and follow up on your way to achieving the outcome? And how will you celebrate the success?

The Innovation Hub will be responsible for measuring progess both during the six months of the initial initiative described here, as well as once the innovative dialogue is up and running. The sponsors are expecting to see regular updates on progress and results.

Sophia and her colleagues in the Innovation Hub will continue their thought leadership and communicate progress and results on a monthly basis to all employees.

They will measure success based on how many employees have got involved in innovative dialogue in the first three months (after kick-off). The goal is to have at least 25 per cent having had some kind of input in that time.

Success will be celebrated through a quarterly innovative thinking award.

How will you make sure you follow through and measure and celebrate success?

This is how I will follow through and follow up:

This is how I will measure success:

This is how I will celebrate success:

THE EFFECT ON CULTURE

An organisation's culture around creativity drives the level of innovation it achieves. A more innovative organisation is much more likely to be more profitable. The extent to which employees are allowed to be creative and innovative influences the culture. If people are allowed to take risks or try new things out, it encourages a culture of innovation. Being blamed and shut down when people make mistakes or things do not go as planned can create a different kind of culture. The innovative culture is driven by everyday behaviours of leaders, once again minute by minute, interaction by interaction. Your behaviour counts.

Now that you have worked your way through how you will lead to achieve innovative impact, you may also want to transfer your notes and create a complete plan by filling in the Impact Roadmap Worksheet at the back of the book or by downloading it from www.2020visionleader.com/ImpactRoadmap.

Self-assessment

Now that you have created your impact Roadmap, please review the progress you have made by completing this self-assessment.

How would you rate your ability to create innovative impact in these areas?

	1 Very poor	2 Poor	3 Just OK	4 Good	5 Excellent
Releasing people's innovative potential					
Driving continuous innovation					
Getting people excited about innovative challenges					

The best way to predict the future is to invent it.

Alan Kay

11
Business sustainability impact

> **LEADERSHIP FACT**
>
> **Did you know?**
>
> Purposeful companies outperform the market by 42 per cent.[36]

Self-assessment

Before reading this chapter, do the following quick self-assessment.

How would you rate your ability to create business sustainability impact?

	1 Very poor	2 Poor	3 Just OK	4 Good	5 Excellent
Raise awareness of business sustainability internally					
Engage employees in sustainable business practices					
Drive sustainable business results					

The case for business sustainability

Business sustainability could mean all sorts of things, so let us clarify what we mean.

We would describe it as being able to deliver results over time, to not just drive for short-term results, but thinking about the long-term effects of decisions, actions and behaviours, to create long-term, sustainable success. We would argue that any organisation would want to secure longevity, to be able to reap the rewards of investments in time, money and effort, over time.

We are all familiar with the concept of the bottom line. It is about financial viability, where decisions need to consider the impact on the bottom line, e.g. *is this action, product, service or investment going to add to the bottom line or subtract from it?* This is clearly of great importance to any organisation as it is not viable to do things that are not going to pay back in some way. So far, we are probably all in agreement. There is, however, growing argument for the consideration of three, rather than just the one, bottom line. This is often described as the Triple P bottom line,[37] where the three Ps stand for people, planet and profits.

So, what does it mean? It means that an organisation that wants to be successful over time (sustainable) and not just in the short term, needs to judge all decisions, actions and habits against these three measures:

▌ What is the impact on *people* (e.g. the human resources: employees, customers, suppliers, other stakeholders, communities where the organisation operates, etc.)?

▌ What is the impact on the *planet* (the earth's natural resources)?

▌ What is the impact on *profit* (the financial resources: the 'regular' bottom line)?

Simply put, you could summarise this as carefully considering and respecting *all* the resources on which you are dependent to run a successful business. The argument is that you need to consider *all* three of these *all* of the time.

The Triple P Bottom Line

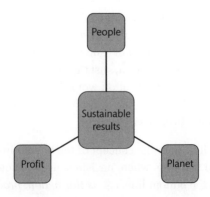

Let us give a simplified example to illustrate this.

Imagine an organisation that is considering outsourcing part of its service to another company, potentially also in another country.

When the company looks at the financial aspect of this decision, it may find that the servicing can be done more cost effectively elsewhere, as salaries are lower, so the impact on *profit* would be positive.

When they look at the *people* impacted, they find that there would obviously be a negative effect on existing employees, a positive effect on the outsourcing company's employees, but potentially also a negative effect on customers if the new service setup lacks in overall knowledge of the company, its products and services. If this is the case, this may, over time, affect customers' experience, loyalty and, ultimately, their spend, which affects *profit* negatively.

When turning their attention to the impact on natural resources, they find that the outsourcing company is much less energy efficient in their office setup, which means more energy is used, depleting energy (*planet*) and costing money (*profit*). There is also greater awareness of energy sustainability in society overall, which means this would have a negative impact on how the company is perceived by key stakeholders (*people*) – which can impact attractiveness negatively in the eyes of potential employees, customers and investors.

In this particular example, the organisation may, therefore, decide not to outsource as the longer-term effect would be negative on all three bottom lines.

As you can see from this simplified example, this is not always a very straightforward process and assessing the long-term impact is not that easy, but it needs to be done just the same. Big investments are made when organisations are set up, and to potentially waste that investment only to meet short-term financial goals is not a viable long-term financial solution.

The three bottom lines are interdependent, they need each other. Focusing too much on one of them, regardless of which one, can have a negative effect on the other(s).

Leaders need to operate continuously with this complexity in mind, to always consider the *impact* of actions on all aspects of business. And, as more and more companies act globally (buy products, services and infrastructure from all over the world, rather than just locally), the complexity grows, it becomes more challenging to assess the impact.

System thinking, being able to assess and understand the greater system you are part of, is therefore a major skill and ability that leaders need. And thinking about the three bottom lines is a good place to start.

Yes, sustainability has become a popular word in business, but few organisations do it well. Business sustainability is to take the big picture view, to consider *all* the complexities of business and to consider the impact of decisions, actions and behaviours – not just in the short term, but also in the mid and long term. It is to think about the impact on the financial, human and natural resources a business needs to succeed. Creating sustainable, long-term success is something all businesses should aim for.

Business sustainability is not just a department, It is a strategy and an attitude.

In our experience, business sustainability is difficult to achieve unless it becomes a part of the organsiation's core:

its culture and its true character. It needs to form part of what the organisation stands for and part of how it makes a difference (to all the resources on which it is dependent – the 3Ps).

The concept of business sustainability is equally relevant for all organisations, from small, independent businesses to large, global corporations. It may get more complex the larger the organisation is, but the principles of long-term focus on careful resource management remain the same.

We are also seeing that businesses are starting to play a larger role in shaping the sustainability agenda for the world, recognising that they have a responsibility for the overall sustainable development of our shared world.

In December 2015, 193 countries came together in the so called 'Paris Agreement', a commitment to United Nations' '2030 Agenda for Sustainable Development' and its 17 Sustainable Development Goals.[38] These goals, which cover environmental, social and economic factors, often are used as guidelines and goals for organisations when they want to contribute to the world's sustainable development and achieve long-term business results.

Sustainable Development Goals

Let us reflect on and create a Roadmap for how to achieve business sustainability impact. These steps include tools and tips to achieve your outcome.

The Business Sustainability Roadmap

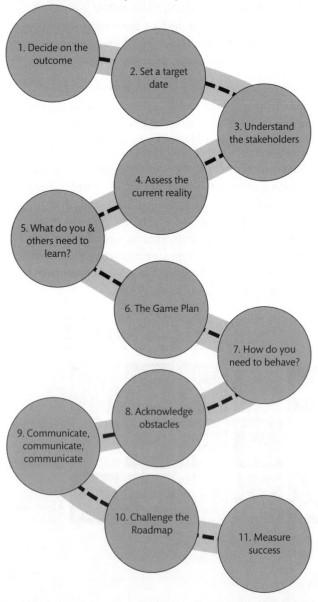

Roadmap step 1: decide on the outcome

So, what is it that you want to achieve? For what purpose do you want to drive business sustainability more effectively? The clearer you can be on this, the more pull it will have on you and the people involved, helping you make choices to move you towards it.

So what could an outcome look like? Let us use an example. We will continue using this example throughout the chapter.

The executive team, which includes Helmut, for quite a while have prided themselves in having a sustainable profile as an organisation. They have become very aware of energy consumption and have, as much as they can, switched to renewable energy sources. Their philanthropy focus is also a source of pride, where the company supports local charities wherever they have offices, while also currently building a school in Malawi and planting trees in Brazil. However, a recent survey has shown that sustainability is largely the responsibility of the sustainability team and a few key sponsors from the executive team.

The executive team has become aware that their sustainability efforts are not necessarily a reflection of a truly sustainable company, which is something they want to become. Helmut is now leading an initiative where the company wants to raise the awareness internally about how important business sustainability is, so that sustainability can become embedded into how they do business, not just how they talk and act externally.

To make sense, any outcome should contribute to the overall vision and purpose of the organisation. There needs to be a red thread from the outcome you identify to each person's part in it. There has to be a compelling reason to drive business sustainability, rather than just 'it's the right thing to do'.

Maybe it is about survival or wanting to portray a sustainability profile to attract investors, partners and employees. A word of advice, though – unless sustainability can become a core belief that people feel passionately about, sustainable practices become tick-box exercises rather than a heartfelt mission, and you are at risk of being seen as 'greenwashing', i.e. just being sustainable on the surface. And that in itself can have a negative impact on the organisation.

> The outcome in this case can be described as: achieving true business sustainability (having sustainable business practices and behaviours embedded through the organisations), securing long-term business success.

Fill in your business sustainability outcome below – why/in what way you want to achieve greater sustainability.

My business sustainability outcome is:

Roadmap step 2: set a target date

By when do you want to achieve this? And if there is not an obvious target date, do you need to create one? Deadlines focus the mind and start an internal clock ticking. Without a clear endpoint, things can drift and procrastination can kick in. What gets measured gets done.

In this chapter's story, Helmut and the executive team have set a target date of two years.

What is your target date? Fill it in here.

The target date is:

Roadmap step 3: understand the stakeholders

Who does this involve and impact? Who are your stakeholders? What do you know and understand about them? What more do you need to know about them?

Helmut feels slightly daunted by the initiative as he starts to think about how many stakeholders this involves. Not only is this an internal affair where all employees are involved, it also touches all their business partners along the supply chain as well as customers, local societies where the company operates and the general public. He smiles wryly to himself when he realises that the multiple stakeholders are a metaphor for sustainability as a whole - that is how complex it is.

The company's employees have not been involved in any sustainability activities, but that has not been expected either.

➤

> Helmut does know that the external supply chain has been worked on for a while and is being continuously reviewed by key individuals within the purchasing and sustainability teams amongst others.
>
> Helmut knows that customers are increasingly asking questions, expecting transparency in their business practices, wanting to see their sustainability credential. Lately, that has also been coming up in job interviews where candidates have asked similar questions as they want to work for a sustainable company.

Through his reflections, Helmut has recognised that the way he and the rest of the executive team approach their stakeholders will make all the difference, and that it starts with being true role models for business sustainability themselves, not just talking about it. This is something he will need to talk about with his peers straightaway.

Helmut is not sure how much employees know about sustainability, so this is something he will need to find out. Having worked on many employee-related initiatives over the years, he is well aware he will need to involve employees across the organisation in the process as early as possible to get their interest and support. When it comes to supply chain partners, he will liaise with purchasing *et al.* to explore those stakeholders more. When it comes to the rest of the external world, expectations from customers and future employees, it is becoming clearer and clearer, but Helmut will also discuss this with HR, customer services and marketing & communications. The greatest focus, however, to start with, will be on employees.

You must stop and reflect on the bigger picture, be strategic and consider each stakeholder individually as well as how they impact each other.

My stakeholders are:

This is what I know about them and their needs:

Please complete your own stakeholder analysis below.

For more in-depth information on stakeholder planning, please go to Chapter 4.

Roadmap step 4: assess the current reality

Be realistic about where you are currently with regard to business sustainability for this specific outcome. Notice the difference between where you are right now and where you want to be (your outcome). How big is the gap? You really need to get a sense of how big or small the gap is so that you can make a realistic assessment of what it will take to close the gap. Do not be judgemental about it, accept the current reality as it is – it is not good, bad, right or wrong.

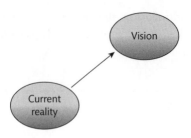

Whenever there is a gap between how things are now and how you want them to be, there is a natural tension that is created in that space. That tension can be described as an elastic band pulled taut between the current and future situation. Unless the desired outcome is strong enough to pull you out of the current reality, you will default back into current reality. So make sure the outcome you are after is very clear and shared with those whom it concerns.

Helmut knows that business sustainability is not embedded in the organisation yet. In fact, it is seen largely as the responsibility of the sustainability team. Having recently talked to a couple of his direct reports to sound them out about the subject, he has become painfully aware that sustainability is not front of mind, even for his own people. The only real sustainable practices that are embedded in people's working day are recycling and some water-saving habits.

Helmut was not really surprised about the distance he could see between their current reality and their outcome, but he was disappointed in himself for not quite realising this earlier. He admits to himself that *a lot* of work needs to get done over the next two years to close the gap.

> In their current reality, business sustainability is seen by employees and leaders as the responsibility of the sustainability team. Sustainability is not seen as something that concerns people on a day-to-day basis, hence companywide sustainability practices are rare.

What does your current reality look like (in contrast to your outcome)? Write it down here.

> Our current reality looks like this:

What are you going to do with that distance, that natural tension that is created between the current reality and the desired outcome? Hold on to any ideas you are having – we will get to action planning in step 6.

Roadmap step 5: what do you and others need to learn?

What do you need to learn (about) to be able to do this? What do your stakeholders need to learn?

Helmut is very interested in the subject of business sustainability and has been reading up on it for some time. The more he has read, the more he has seen the possibilities in making it part of the company's DNA. The more he has learnt, the more he has also come to understand that there is so much more he needs to learn, not just to convey knowledge to others but to create his own sustainable habits so that his mission does not just become a theoretical one.

Helmut assesses that employees may have very varying understanding of business sustainability, but that, overall, the learning need is big.

Helmut decides that he will create a structured learning plan for himself to fast-forward his learning. He also sees that employees and leaders need a similar learning plan, where the focus for leaders will also be on how to lead sustainability and sustainable practices.

What learnings are needed for you and your stakeholders? Capture your observations below.

This is what I need to learn about:

This is what my stakeholders need to learn about:

Roadmap step 6: the Game Plan

What needs doing?
Who will do it?
When will it be done?

This step can help trigger your thoughts on what specific decisions and actions you and your organisation need to take to achieve your specific business sustainability outcome. As this is a big and constantly evolving subject, keep your eyes peeled and find the latest research, articles, books, sustainability forums and groups that can give you the specific information and insights you need. Consider the '2030 Agenda'[39] and its 17 sustainable development goals in your research and as a starting point for internal dialogue.

As you now bring together your thoughts from steps 1–5, here are a few possible suggestions for your Game Plan, to move you into action.

Involve people from the start

A sustainability agenda is a big culture change and, as such, needs everyone involved. Think through in what forums you can bring people together, online or face to face. Consider what input you want to have from them, and craft a number of questions that can lead that dialogue. Here are some examples:

▌ What does sustainability mean to you?

▌ What ideas do you have for how we can become more sustainable?

▌ What challenges do you see and how could we overcome them?

▌ What would be a really great outcome for you with all of this? What matters to you?

Educate people on sustainability

It is a big subject so just talking to people about it is most likely not going to be enough. Seek out existing development programmes, online learning, books, podcasts and more. Whatever learning path you choose, make sure it is tangible enough and that you can add an organisation-specific element to it where employees can discuss, explore and apply what they learn in real life, at work. In finding the right way to educate, consider this:

▌ Who has successfully done this before, what did they do, how did they educate?

▌ What format will work best for us? Online? Self-studies? Discussion forums?

▌ How can we make the learning sustainable over time? Regular, short modules at work as reminders?

▌ Could we educate experts internally who could train and coach others?

▌ What do leaders need to learn to be able to *lead* sustainability?

Create a value proposition

What will be the benefits of your business sustainability focus? Your stakeholders will want to know. Spend time working out the value proposition to all of this: what difference it will make, what value it will give *people, planet* and *profit* – the three bottom lines. A clear value proposition will be key to all communication going forward.

Build on this impact assessor when making decisions to assess the short- and long-term impact on *people, planet* and *profit,* from the planned actions.

To do/action	Short-term impact +/-			
	People		Planet	Profit
	Employees	Customer		

To do/action	Long-term impact +/-			
	People		Planet	Profit
	Employees	Customer		

Manage expectations

A very tangible way of making sure that you are making progress is to start putting together short-, mid- and, long-term goals with most focus on the long-term. Results may not be seen right away and, therefore, quarterly results evaluation may not be the most efficient way of presenting the results of a sustainable strategy. Therefore, it is of importance to explain to shareholders and other stakeholders that there will come a time when this will pay off, but they are not going to see the result right away. Leaders should not be afraid of growing that influence where they can confidently talk about the result and the strategic choice.

Be realistic and stay focused

Business sustainability is, indeed, a big area and, once you start looking outside, thinking about all the ways that you could make a difference, it is easy to become distracted and overwhelmed. And, when people get overwhelmed, they tend to give up. For that reason, stay focused on what is closest to the organisation's overall purpose, focusing on where you can make a difference there. Focus on the things you can control first, like engaging with your employees, reviewing work processes and changing non-sustainable internal habits.

It is always better to do something than nothing.

Helmut has done a lot of thinking around the Game Plan already as he is a 'doer' and has been thinking about the practicalities for a long time. He has been doing research on what other companies have done to engage their stakeholders and he has also looked at learning programmes for employees. When sustainability had been discussed with the board previously, there have been concerns about the short-term financial implications of a more sustainable focus.

Getting to specific actions that show people exactly what will happen and when makes it easier for people to decide to get involved. Visions and ideas can be exciting but, unless they are practical too, it is difficult to get support for them.

Helmut decides to involve employees from the start, running focus groups to engage in dialogue to kick-start the process, using the 17 sustainable development goals as a practical discussion starter. He will also move ahead and secure the right education programme early on. Helmut needs to think carefully about the value proposition and how that can be used to balance short- and long-term results and manage stakeholders' expectations.

Complete your Game Plan below.

What to do	How to do it	Who will do it	When it will get done	What impact will this have on sustainability?

Roadmap step 7: how do you need to behave?

How do you need to behave? How will those behaviours make others feel so that they want to engage with the sustainability agenda and take on sustainable business practices in their day-to-day work?

Here are a few factors to consider.

It starts with you. What are you role modelling? Are your habits displaying a true spirit of sustainability? What do people see you doing and do those behaviours reflect what you say about sustainability?

The solutions you have identified in your Game Plan work best when carried out with supporting 'how to' behaviours. The actions on their own will take you so far. With the right behaviours, you walk the talk and your business sustainability impact is greater.

As mentioned earlier, good intentions are not enough. Unless sustainability is seen in the decisions you make and how you behave, it will be seen as 'greenwashing', which undermines the ambition and can greatly delay the outcome.

Give hope

When there is time pressure to deliver, people often get worried about the change and the risk of failure. A key leadership attribute, therefore, is to give people hope at such times. The ability to draw a metaphorical picture of the future, a compelling vision of something better, stronger, more lasting, more promising. People need to experience hope of something better at the end of the road and this is where you come in – this is what you, as their leader, can give them. If you are expecting people to really commit themselves to a vision and mission, you need to give them that sense of hope and excitement.

And that hope starts within you. It is near impossible to instil hope if you are not experiencing it yourself. You need to put yourself in a hopeful state of mind of what business sustainability will lead to. These reflective questions can form the foundation for that state:

▌ What are the opportunities in this? How will it change things for the better?

▌ What tangible changes are you looking for? And how will they make a difference for the future?

▌ What might be the challenges and how could they be overcome?

▌ What previous situations have you led through that brought about unexpected benefits (beyond what you had hoped or planned for)?

The choice of words in the questions themselves, and in your answers, matter. Look, for example, at the first bullet points where it says: 'How *will* it change things for the better?' The word *will* assumes that things *will* be better, not that they *could* or *might*, but that they *will.* By using that particular word, you are planting the assumption in your own mind that it definitely *will* be better. And, as long as that assumption is not absurd, (which it should not be or you would not pursue it), your mind will take it in, believe in it and start acting in accordance to make it happen.

You are in charge of making that hope a reality, starting with yourself. Then you can take that hope with you and not just talk about it to people around you, but truly embody it.

Here are some other sustainability behaviours to consider.

▌ Be consistent in words and actions, have a great 'say-do ratio' (this goes for your personal life as well).

▌ Be authentic (never 'greenwash'!).

▌ Be inclusive and open to collaboration across the society you exist in (as sustainability challenges are best worked at across business, government, non-profit organisations, *etc*)

▌ Show your commitment by staying focused, reminding people about the why and how of business sustainability.

On his way to a meeting, Helmut overheard two people who were standing by the window overlooking the car park.

'Oh, look at that!' one of them exclaimed. 'I thought Peter was all for being "green" and that, talking so much about how important it is to think about sustainability, but look at his car!'

The other person nodded: 'I know! That's a real gas guzzler, isnt' it? What was he thinking! Nice car, of course, but he obviously isn't as concerned about fossil fuel and sustainability as he's been letting on.'

> Helmut knows that it is going to be crucial for him to be consistent and authentic in how he leads this organisational focus on business sustainability. This is not foreign to him, he would like to think that he would do that anyway, but he is becoming more and more aware that it might be particularly important in this case.

So, how do you choose to behave to drive sustainability in your business?

This is how I choose to behave	This is how each of these behaviours will have an impact on the steps of my Game Plan

Roadmap step 8: acknowledge obstacles

What obstacles are there? Or could there be? How can they be overcome?

Here are some examples of obstacles to business sustainability that we often observe in organisations:

▍ People not engaging with the sustainability agenda as sustainability is seen as 'somebody else's responsibility' (e.g. the sustainability team).

We recently carried out a small survey, inviting 40 leaders from different organisations (within the same industry) all around the world to share their sustainability practices. The majority of them (about 70 per cent) reported a high-level sustainability focus within the organisation as a whole but very little, if anything, affected them in their job. This result suggests that sustainability is often perceived by employees as not being a core aspect of the organisation's being or, indeed, a shared responsibility for everyone.

▌ Sustainability is complex and this makes it hard to grasp – *where to start?*

▌ Short-term financial reporting leads to short-term decisions, contra-productive to long-term, sustainable outcomes. Unless organisations can show shareholders that decisions are made that will give return on investment over time (even if not in the short term), they may jeopardise financial backing. This could be true for any industry while sustainability grows in importance, acceptance and understanding.

▌ Lack of time

In a recent town hall meeting in the head office, the head of sustainability reported on great energy saving results for the offices around the world. Helmut noticed that, overall, people listened, but in a distant 'this is great, but it doesn't really concern me' kind of way, with several people glancing at mobile phones or having quiet side conversations with their colleague next to them while she was talking.

As Helmut now reflects on that meeting and what he has experienced since getting involved in the business sustainability mission, he concludes that people feel distant from the whole subject, not directly touched by it or involved in it. It is something that happens 'elsewhere'.

> Helmut assessed that the main obstacle is that employees do not see sustainability as their responsibility and, even if they did, they would not know what that meant or how they could get involved. Another possible obstacle could be lack of time; everyone is busy as it is, so asking for people's commitment may just feel like getting 'yet another thing to do'.

What obstacles do you see that need overcoming – for you, the team(s), the organisation?

The obstacles I can foresee:

How I will overcome them:

Roadmap step 9: communicate, communicate, communicate

What will you communicate? Who, when, how, to whom?
How do you need to be and behave in your communication?

When thinking about communication for a specific outcome, there are often two aspects of two-way communication that need particular attention.

The first one is *framing* – how will you frame the message overall, particularly when you first share it? Framing is very much about how you communicate, the words you use, the stories you tell, the way you help people see the importance in what you are saying. It is about communicating a message in such a way that you influence people to listen to you. How are you building in a feedback loop so you can get immediate input from those involved?

The second one is the structure and determination of ongoing progress and results communication needed to keep people motivated and help them see the progress made. Typically, this would involve frequency, method, channel and feedback loop.

As Helmut's main focus is on getting employees engaged and passionate about the business sustainability mission, this is the communication he will focus on most. He recognises that he will, of course, also work with the rest of the executives and their functions, including the marketing & communications team and the sustainability team to work on communication with external stakeholders.

Helmut identifies the following key messages that employees will benefit from hearing and being reminded of:

▌ By putting sustainability at the heart of our business strategy, we are creating value not just for ourselves but for the world we live in and depend on. This can guarantee our survival for the future.

> ▌ This is how you can get involved and make a difference . . .
>
> ▌ This is what we will do . . .
>
> ▌ This is why we think sustainability is so important . . .

What do you want your stakeholders to hear? Fill in the speech bubbles below.

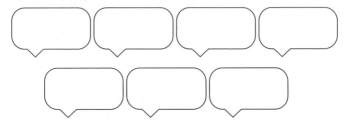

Roadmap step 10: challenge the Roadmap

Challenge your draft impact Roadmap – how could you think of all of this differently?

OK, let us question everything one more time. What if there was another way to achieve this business sustainability outcome? Review what you have reflected on so far and ask yourself – how could I think of all this differently? Could there be a completely different approach to drive sustainable business results effectively?

Leave it for a day and review again	Ask a friend!
Talk to a peer	Talk to your team

Look at it from a new perspective by imagining yourself as someone else–a few examples below (imagine how they would look and sound)–what would they do?
Elon Musk
Your main competitor in the industry
Arnold Schwarzenegger
A customer
A charity like Cancer Research
Or someone else!

Or are there any additional ideas that you want to add to your plan so far?

> When challenging my current thinking, this is what I come up with:

Roadmap step 11: measure the success

How are you going to measure your business sustainability outcome? How will you know if you have achieved the kind of progress and results you were aiming for? How will you ensure you follow through and follow up on your way to achieving the outcome? And how will you celebrate the success?

Helmut and his peers on the executive team sat around their meeting table, discussing how to keep the momentum going for their business sustainability ambitions.

Helmut said: 'We need to lead the way here. We have to be consistent and practise what we preach when it comes to sustainability.' The others nodded.

He then added: 'You know what it's like – what gets measured gets done. We need to goal people on sustainability; it needs to become a key business measure for us going forward.
I know we don't know yet exactly how those goals are best formulated, but they will evolve over time and we can start with what we know.'

Helmut will follow up through regular sustainability check-ins (mainly online) with employees and the executive team will have business sustainability on their agenda for every meeting going forward.

Success will be measured through feedback from employees as well as the specific indicators and goals for each business area, once the sustainability potential has been assessed in each area.

Helmut is mainly planning for frequent, small celebrations and recognitions, delegated to frontline leaders, to keep the momentum going.

How will you make sure you follow through and measure and celebrate success?

This is how I will follow through and follow up:

This is how I will measure success:

This is how I will celebrate success:

THE EFFECT ON CULTURE

When you start to focus on long-term results, as well as short-term ones, you start to shift the 'way things get done around here', the culture. The culture becomes one where people are more aware of how everything is connected and how decisions impact results in the long term. And, when you take it back to the values of the workforce, considering generational and diversity differences, you engage people through purpose. Sustainability is more important to some audiences than you may realise, so it can help make the culture a magnet for talent too. Be sincere, make sure you really believe in it. Focus on the aspects that you enjoy and believe in and then talk about that with passion and feeling. It is infectious. Now *that* is a recipe for a successful culture of business sustainability.

Your impact is your legacy

Now that you have worked your way through how you will lead to achieve business sustainability impact, you may also want to transfer your notes and create a complete plan by filling in the Impact Roadmap Worksheet at the back of the book or by downloading it from www.2020visionleader.com/ImpactRoadmap.

Self-assessment

Now that you have created your impact Roadmap, please review the progress you have made by completing this self-assessment.

How would you rate your ability to create business sustainability impact?

	1 Very poor	2 Poor	3 Just OK	4 Good	5 Excellent
Raise awareness of business sustainability internally					
Engage employees in sustainable business practices					
Drive sustainable business results					

To be truly successful, companies need to have a corporate mission that is bigger than making a profit.

Marc Benioff

Summary

This book is all about you and how you can take greater control of your impact on people and the world around you, to create good working relationships, great teams, healthy work cultures and sustainable organisational results.

What ideas did *you* pick up and how will you put them into practice?

As a quick reference and reminder, here are the main concepts, solutions, tools and the behaviours that are explored in each chapter.

Chapter 1: What is impact?

- Impact starts from within
- Your impact is about the ripple effect you create
- Creating an impact strategy
- Impact through position alone or through behaviour?
- Taking responsibility for your impact
- Understanding your audience
- Being authentic and using your ULPs
- How actions and behaviours drive impact
- Research on leadership impact

Chapter 2: The why and how of achieving impact

▌ Reasons to focus on impact

▌ Impact happens in the moment

▌ What goes with the title?

▌ The way you behave and your habits

▌ Being a great communicator and listener

▌ ULPs – unique leadership points

▌ Leadership Radar – being really aware

▌ Impact and company culture

Chapter 3: Impact on employees

▌ Have a vision and carry it through

▌ Treat people as individuals and value differences

▌ Get teams to believe in themselves

▌ Be authentic, take off your corporate cloak

▌ Be intentional about your brand and reputation

Behaviours

▌ Engaging and caring acknowledgement of employee's accomplishment

▌ Thinking carefully about how to position the vision with people in mind

▌ Talking openly and expressing oneself, being passionate

Chapter 4: Impact on people more senior than you

▌ Stakeholder leadership

▌ Stakeholder influencing

- Use organic and reverse mentoring
- Be your own brand manager
- Prepare for meetings – how to be

Behaviours

- Volunteering information and daring to share a bold idea
- Asking questions and listening intently
- Sharing observations and allowing for others to confirm those thoughts

Chapter 5: Impact on people at the same level (peers)

- Treat your peers like customers
- Be generous with credit, stingy with blame
- Give peer-to-peer observations
- Be politically aware
- Seek out learning opportunities with your peers

Behaviours

- Looking for solutions
- Explaining why including me is so helpful – for us both
- Generous sharing

Chapter 6: Impact on the board of directors

Executive presence as an impact tool

- Demonstrating confidence
- Inspiring and relating
- Communicating and coaching

▌ Relating to vision and strategy

▌ Showing respect

Behaviours

▌ Active engagement, asking board members what they need

▌ Creatively challenging the status quo

▌ Appreciating differences, trying something new

Chapter 7: External impact with stakeholders, media/press, social media

▌ Choosing behaviours that make the difference

▌ Considering your impact on customers and their experience

▌ Working effectively with your partners, suppliers, sub-contractors

▌ Managing the media/press

▌ Social media and brand management

Behaviours

▌ Listening and interacting with an open mind

▌ Choosing to step back and carefully choosing how to engage online

▌ Taking time to choose a response, building a good relationship for next time

Chapter 8: Collaborative impact

▌ Conflict management

▌ Creating a team with the team formula

　▌ Get together as a team

　▌ Get to know each other

▌ Really talk to each other openly

▌ Give each other behavioural TOP feedback™

▌ Build on strengths

▌ Agree on team purpose and direction

▌ Decide how to work together and measure success

▌ Be generous, fearlessly share what you know

▌ Commit to what has been agreed

▌ Keep your promise, hold each other accountable

Behaviours

▌ Being accepting (of self and others)

▌ Being curious

▌ Being respectful

▌ Being genuinely interested in people

▌ Being generous, share what you know

▌ Giving credit when it is due

▌ Letting go of the need to 'be right'

▌ Keeping your promises (being trustworthy)

Chapter 9: Change-driving Impact

▌ Change leadership, not just change management

▌ As a leader, how are you adding value?

▌ The emotional aspect of change

▌ Use the positive change influencers

▌ Do not waste time in 'uncertainty void'

▌ Slow down to speed up the change

▌ No one has all the answers

▌ Hold regular change meetings

Behaviours

▌ Being proactive

▌ Being reflective

▌ Demonstrating responsibility

▌ Being positive

▌ Showing empathy

▌ Being considerate

▌ Being trustworthy

▌ Being sensible

▌ Not being afraid to be courageous

▌ Being open-minded

▌ Demonstrating belief in the change

▌ Most importantly, stopping to celebrate the success you have created

Chapter 10: Innovative impact

▌ The 5 agile steps for disruptive leaders:

   ▌ Build your strategic ability

   ▌ Leave your ego at the door

   ▌ Take teaming and collaboration to a new level

   ▌ Give enough stability so people can act with agility

   ▌ Think H2H – human to human

▌ Build innovation confidence

▌ Run PODS™

▌ Run internal and/or external hackathons

▌ Use conflict to drive innovation

▌ Go and find the problems or opportunities – and start innovating

Behaviours

▊ Being curious

▊ Being inclusive and generous

▊ Being relentlessly customer-centric

▊ Thinking long-term

▊ Being courageous and resilient

▊ Coaching for innovation

Chapter 11: Business sustainability impact

▊ The Triple Bottom Lines: people, planet, profit

▊ Involve people from the start

▊ Educate people on sustainability

▊ Create a value proposition

▊ Manage expectations

▊ Be realistic and stay focused

▊ Give hope

Behaviours

▊ Being consistent in words and actions, have a great 'say-do ratio' (this goes for your personal life as well)

▊ Being authentic (never 'greenwash'!)

▊ Being inclusive and open to collaboration across the society you exist in (as sustainability challenges are best worked at across business, government, non-profit organisations, *etc*)

▊ Showing your commitment by staying focused, reminding people about the why and how of business sustainability

Impact Roadmap Template

		My outcome is		
1	Decide on the outcome			
2	Set a target date	The target date is		
3	Understand the stakeholders	My stakeholders are	This is what I know about them and their needs	
4	Assess the current reality	Our current reality looks like this		

5	What do you and others need to learn?	This is what I need to learn about		This is what my stakeholders need to learn about		
6	The Game Plan	What to do	How to do it	Who will do it	When it will get done	What impact this will have on the outcome
7	How do you need to behave?	This is how I choose to behave		This is how each of these behaviours will have an impact on the steps of my Game Plan		

8	Acknowledge obstacles	The obstacles I can foresee	How I will overcome them	
9	Communicate, communicate, communicate	Key messages I want to get across to my stakeholders		
10	Challenge the Roadmap	When challenging my current thinking, this is what I come up with		
11	Measure the success	This is how I will follow through and follow up	This is how I will measure success	This is how I will celebrate success

Notes

Part 1

Chapter 1

1. https://www.octanner.com/content/dam/oc-tanner/documents/global-research/White_Paper_Performance_Accelerated.pdf.

2. https://hbr.org/2016/01/the-trickle-down-effect-of-good-and-bad-leadership.

3. http://www.haygroup.com/Downloads/es/misc/Leadership_brochure.pdf.

4. http://news.gallup.com/businessjournal/182792/managers-account-variance-employee-engagement.aspx.

5. http://news.gallup.com/businessjournal/163130/employee-engagement-drives-growth.aspx.

Chapter 2

6. http://www.bandt.com.au/opinion/five-reasons-emotional-intelligence-essential-effective-leadership.

7. http://www.apa.org/research/action/multitask.aspx.

Part 2

Chapter 3

8. https://www.theguardian.com/careers/careers-blog/
what-employees-want-job-company-around-world.

9. http://news.gallup.com/businessjournal/182792/
managers-account-variance-employee-engagement.aspx.

10. http://www.loni.usc.edu/.

Chapter 4

11. https://hbr.org/2015/12/
engaging-your-employees-is-good-but-dont-stop-there.

12. https://greatergood.berkeley.edu/article/item/
how_stories_change_brain.

13. http://www.loni.usc.edu/.

Chapter 5

14. https://www.gallup.com/workplace/236570/employees-
lot-managers.aspx.

15. https://www.mckinsey.com/business-functions/
organization/our-insights/the-five-trademarks-of-agile-
organizations.

16. https://hbr.org/2017/09/
playing-office-politics-without-selling-your-soul.

17. http://www.loni.usc.edu/.

18. https://www.ddiworld.com/glf2018.

Chapter 6

19. http://www.debonogroup.com/six_thinking_hats.php.

20. http://www.loni.usc.edu/.

21. https://www.thetimes.co.uk/article/same-old-story-from-the-boardroom-as-average-age-of-directors-exceeds-60-jb6s0x3dn.

22. https://ig.ft.com/sites/us-board-diversity/.

Chapter 7

23. https://www.webershandwick.com/news/81-percent-of-global-executives-report-external-ceo-engagement-is-a-mandate/.

24. https://www.inc.com/justin-bariso/uber-ceo-single-insulting-tweet-destroy-months-work-major-lesson-emotional-intelligence.html.

25. http://www.loni.usc.edu/.

Part 3

Chapter 8

26. https://www.nytimes.com/2016/02/28/magazine/what-google-learned-from-its-quest-to-build-the-perfect-team.html.

27. https://www.forbes.com/sites/adigaskell/2017/06/22/new-study-finds-that-collaboration-drives-workplace-performance/#636dd6053d02.

28. Published by MX Publishing, 2013.

Chapter 9

29. https://www.ddiworld.com/glf/gender-diversity-pays-off.

30. https://www.youtube.com/watch?v=W8lBMFw2xFA.

31. https://hbr.org/2018/08/research-to-get-people-to-embrace-change-emphasize-what-will-stay-the-same?utm_medium=social&utm_source=twitter&utm_campaign=hbr.

Chapter 10

32. https://www.octanner.com/in/insights/infographics/the-business-case-for-recognition.html.

33. https://www.mckinsey.com/business-functions/organization/our-insights/the-five-trademarks-of-agile-organizations.

34. https://hbr.org/2018/07/the-biggest-obstacles-to-innovation-in-large-companies.

35. http://blessingwhite.com/article/2018/04/20/7-barriers-internal-innovation/.

Chapter 11

36. https://www.ddiworld.com/glf2018.

37. Term coined by John Elkington, founder of the consulting firm SustainAbility.

38. https://www.un.org/sustainabledevelopment/development-agenda/.

39. https://www.un.org/sustainabledevelopment/sustainable-development-goals/.

Index

Additional resources

The authors have written two other, award-winning books, detailed below.

Leading Teams: 10 Challenges 10 Solutions published by FT Publishing, 2015

ISBN-10: 1292083085

Packed full of valuable advice and powerful techniques, *Leading Teams* has something practical to offer everyone – whatever your level. Covering 10 of the most common team challenges, this book gives you proven solutions to ensure your team delivers consistent and lasting results. Look inside and discover how to build trust, boost team morale, overcome conflict, create engagement and manage change effectively, ensuring your team reaches its full potential. Whether you are looking to solve a particular team challenge or just want to make sure you're taking the right approach, this book will show you how.

The Team Formula: The Leadership Tale of a Team Who Found their Way published by MX publishing, 2013

ISBN-10: 1780923473

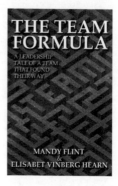

This is a business book told in a story format for leaders: a leadership tale. The story takes place in the world of international business where, as a result of acquisition, two companies merge, creating a disparate team that is struggling with change. Stephen, as the leader of the team, is struggling to get them to work effectively and efficiently together. In these times of economic change, it is more important than ever that he gets it right. Follow Stephen and his team on their journey though the thorny maze that all teams travel through. This is a quick must-read.

Other resources

On our website www.2020visionleader.com, you can find a number of models and exercises from the book and additional resources, including:

▌ Stakeholder plan/map

▌ TOP Feedback™

▌ Personal brand exercise

▌ EQ exercise

▌ Impact Roadmap